In Search

of the

Seven Wonders
of Wales

Eirwen Shelbourne

bridge
books

In Search of the Seven Wonders of Wales
first published in Wales in 2010
by
BRIDGE BOOKS
61 Park Avenue
Wrexham
LL12 7AW

ISBN 978-1-84494-063-9

Printed and bound
by
Cromwell Press Group,
Trowbridge, Wiltshire

In memory of
my late partner
David

Contents

Acknowledgements

I AM DEEPLY GRATEFUL to my late partner, David, for his constant support and encouragement and willingness, at all times, to drive me to the various 'wonders'. His companionship during our many walks in the various villages and their churches, along canal and river banks, steep hills and mountain paths, proved to be invaluable.

My interest in and love of photography was nurtured many years ago by two friends – Gwyneth and Emrys Jones — whose expertise and enthusiasm resulted in my taking up a hobby which I still enjoy. For this I am most grateful.

I would also like to thank all those who freely give of their time to care for the many places I have visited during the research for this book. Without their constant support and vigilance many of the hidden gems encountered on this 'journey' would have long since disappeared.

Finally, my gratitude to Alister Williams of Bridge Books for his encouragement and support throughout the publishing process.

Eirwen Shelbourne
2010

Introduction

HAVING LIVED IN NORTH-EAST WALES for over thirty years, it was no surprise that I soon became aware of the 'Seven Wonders of Wales' as recorded by an anonymous eighteenth century poet:

Pistyll Rhaeadr and Wrexham steeple,
Snowdon's mountain without its people,
Overton Yew trees, St Winifred's Well,
Llangollen Bridge and Gresford bells.

On first reading this rhyme, I was intrigued as to the name of the author and why all the 'wonders' listed, with the exception of Snowdon Mountain, were confined to north-east Wales. In spite of persistent research, the author's name has not come to light. Many have said that this old rhyme is nothing but a nonsense, probably penned by some eighteenth century north Walian 'wag' who had not travelled beyond his home territory and just wanted to score some points, as it were, over his compatriots in mid and south Wales. A rather vague suggestion, however, points to the possibility that the author was a north Walian whose work entailed travelling through the areas where his 'seven wonders' are situated and they became familiar landmarks to him. It is also a well-known fact that the number seven has been prominent in religion and folk-tradition over the centuries, and the author could well have been influenced by this, together with an awareness of the 'Seven Wonders' of the ancient world. Travelling was very much in vogue during the eighteenth and early nineteenth centuries, whether taking on the 'Grand Tour' of Europe or touring around the natural wonders, viewing the architectural splendours or taking the waters at the holy places of one's native land. It did not really matter. Simply seeing such places did much to enhance one's social standing. During this period, many travellers passed through north Wales en route to Ireland from London. With the completion of Telford's London–Holyhead road, there was a marked increase in the number of early 'tourists' and the author of the rhyme could well have been one such tourist who composed his verse in order to boast to his friends that he had visited the 'Seven Wonders of Wales'. There is no doubt that the majority of places listed in the rhyme have never been considered tourist 'hotspots' and would only have attracted a specific type of traveller. It is only Snowdon, in all its splendour, that has been a major attraction over the centuries.

Having visited the 'Seven Wonders of Wales', I felt that each one justified the trouble taken to seek it out and had its own wondrous appeal, whether it be natural beauty, architectural masterpiece or religious influence. I also found that the areas around the 'wonders', and the routes from one 'wonder' to the next, had their own interesting tales to tell. It is my hope that this book will encourage visitors to north Wales, and specifically to north-east Wales, to visit the 'old Seven Wonders'. The journey between them will provide an insight into the history, traditions and culture of the area and reveal some hidden gems of nature and man's ingenuity. Although my journey does not follow the sequence as recorded in the rhyme, any one of them can be chosen as a starting point. For the visitor with limited time, several of the 'wonders' can be visited in one day as the distance between them is not too great. Whichever choice of route is taken, there is no doubt it will provide an opportunity to enjoy the unspoilt countryside around Pistyll Rhaeadr, the vibrant town bustling around Wrexham's steeple, the tranquility surrounding the old Yew trees at Overton, the sound of Gresford's Bells resounding over the village rooftops, the rush of the deep waters of the River Dee below Llangollen Bridge, the peacefulness of St Winifred's Well and, finally, the exhilaration of climbing to Snowdon's summit.

Wonder 1

Oswestry – Llansilin – PISTYLL RHAEADR – Llanrhaeadr-ym-Mochnant – Ceiriog Valley – Chirk

PISTYLL RHAEADR IS SITUATED right on the southern boundary of the County Borough of Wrexham, on the border of Powys, and a few miles from the village of Llanrhaeadr-ym-Mochnant. Access to this remote corner from either north or south Wales, or from over the English border, is via the market town of Oswestry in Shropshire which is situated very near to the Welsh border and to the A5, one of the main highways bringing visitors into Wales.

Often referred to as the 'Oswestry Borderland', this area has over centuries been both Welsh and English and this is echoed in its rich heritage. Due to its close proximity to Wales, it has become a focal point for the inhabitants across the border, particularly farmers on market day, when the language of the town becomes Welsh, so much so that visitors think they have arrived in Wales. The town straddles an ancient highway, Ffordd Saeson, a prehistoric trade route linking Anglesey with the river Severn and used by Irish axe traders. Legend has it that the town we see today grew up around St Oswald's Well, named after King Oswald of Northumbria, who was defeated in battle here by the Mercian King Penda in 642. According to legend, Oswald was killed and his body cruelly dismembered and hung on the branches of a tree. A passing eagle swooped down and carried off one of the dismembered arms but soon dropped it. A spring gushed out at the spot where the arm fell, becoming known as St Oswald's Well, which became a place of pilgrimage because of the reputed healing properties of the waters. An alternative story, however, suggests that the tree from which the dead king's body was hanged was referred to as 'Oswald's Tree' which, over time, became

Oswestry. Whichever legend one chooses to believe, it confirms the fact that Oswestry has an interesting, if at times a very turbulent past.

Research shows that the town's history goes back further than even King Oswald, for situated on the outskirts of the town is the huge and impressive Iron Age hill fort of Hen Ddinas. Now known as 'Old Oswestry', it is one of the finest of its kind in the borderland. Constant border disputes have, however, left their mark on the town and surrounding areas. As far back as the eighth century, a massive defensive ditch with ramparts known as Wat's Dyke was constructed which stretched from the Dee estuary in the north to Morda Bank, south of Oswestry. Remnants of it can still be seen today at various places along its path. At a later stage, in a further effort to hold back the marauding Welsh, King Offa of Mercia constructed Offa's Dyke which stretches for 160 miles from the north Wales coast to the Severn estuary. Lying to the west of the town, this remarkable construction is walkable for most of its length.

With the coming of the Normans, Oswestry gained in importance because of its strategic border position. A motte and bailey castle was constructed in an effort to quell the raiding Welsh. Unfortunately, only fragments of its walls are left to the north-west of the town off the B4580 road. The town was granted a borough charter in 1228 and flourished as a market centre, becoming one of the most important of the Marcher lordships and for many centuries, despite being the centre of English government, was more Welsh than English. Throughout the Middle Ages, Oswestry prospered but this prosperity was regularly interrupted by the Welsh laying claim to the borderland which resulted in the town being destroyed by fire in 1215 (during the time of King John) and later by Prince Llewelyn ap Iorwerth. During the turbulent period of Owain Glyndŵr, who in 1400 led the Welsh in a war of independence, the Welsh captured Oswestry. Glyndŵr and his forces were eventually quelled and a relative peace was maintained until the outbreak of the Civil War in 1644. Unfortunately, the great plague of 1559 killed nearly one third of the town's population. The Croeswylan Stone, also referred to as the Cross of Weeping, reminds us today of this horrific loss of life and can be seen on Morda Road (the A483), on the south side of the town.

During the Civil War, Oswestry was a Royalist stronghold and soon

The remains of the motte, upon which the Norman keep once stood. [ES]

became a target for the Parliamentary army. After a long siege the town was captured and Oliver Cromwell ordered the complete demolition of the castle as a reprisal and all that remains of the castle today can be seen on the top of Castle Bank which has now been transformed into a public park and is well worth a visit to get a good view of the town.

As a result of conflict over many centuries, Oswestry cannot boast many old buildings The church of St Oswald's is very impressive and although its origins go back to Norman times, very little of this early church remain, most of it being in the massive tower which was rebuilt in the 1690s. The rest of the church underwent a major restoration by G. E. Street, between 1872 and 1874. Today's church boasts a splendid porch with carved figures of Christ, Mary and St Oswald. Entrance to the church is through a beautiful doorway of thirteenth century design, the fine oak door with its flower hinges opens into an impressive interior full of interesting features which include a war memorial designed by Sir Giles Gilbert Scott, the architect of Liverpool's Anglican Cathedral, and a memorial to Hugh Yale, a relative of Elihu Yale the benefactor of Yale University in America (the latter is buried in Wrexham).

Another of Oswestry's old surviving buildings is Holbache House, adjacent to the church. Passing out of the churchyard through the

St Oswald's Church, Oswestry. [ES]

Griddlegate, a type of lych-gate deriving its name from a 'grille' in the long-since vanished door, the timbered frame of Holbache House continues to impress. Dating from the 1400s this fine brick and timber building now houses the Oswestry Heritage Centre. In its early days this was a free grammar school founded in 1407 by Welshman David Holbache. This was a pioneering concept at a time when schools were usually attached to a church or monastery. Holbache was Crown Pleader and Attorney for Wales, in addition to being War Treasurer to King Henry IV (who fought against Owain Glyndŵr). Much of the building that has survived is thought to date from Holbache's time, although there are signs of later renovations. When the school outgrew itself it was moved in 1776 to its present site in Upper Brook Street. Holbache House was used as the town workhouse for a period and then as private dwellings until well into the 1950s. In 1984, after a great deal of repair and renovation, the building gained a Civic Trust Award becoming the town's Heritage Centre and Museum.

The exhibits now housed within Holbache House are many and varied and reflect many aspects of Oswestry's history. One room, the Old Schoolroom, has a bench on which pupils carved their names and creates a vivid impression of the type of education promoted centuries ago. Another section of the building is given over to Wilfred Owen, M.C., the Great War poet, born in 1893 in Plas Wilmot on Weston Lane, the son of a railwayman. Tragically, Owen was killed in France just one week before the Armistice in 1918. His legacy of poems relating to the horrors of war have influenced many and emphasise the futility of such action. Despite their topic and content, some say his style and rhythm are reminiscent of Keats. His poems showed a promise of greater things to come.

Also born in Oswestry was Sir Henry Walford Davies (1869–1941). An organist, composer and broadcaster he was Professor of Music at Aberystwyth University and Master of the King's Music. Many visitors to Oswestry are not aware that Edward Lhuyd (1660–1709), the famous botanist and historian, was the illegitimate son of Edward Lloyd of Llanforda, a large estate on the outskirts of Oswestry, where he was brought up. In deference to his Welsh mother, who came from west Wales, he chose to use the old Celtic spelling of his name. Educated at

Oswestry School, he later went to Oxford where his intellectual abilities were further stimulated. It was here that he began a study of the Welsh language, leading him to a consuming interest in all things Celtic. This interest led to the publication in 1707 of his *Archaeologia Britannica*, a massive volume of data relating to the natural history, archaeology, customs and beliefs of every known Celtic community. Amongst his other talents was his skill in recognising rare plants. In Snowdonia, he discovered the 'Snowdon Lily', a flower new to science at that time and given the botanical name *'Serotina Lloydia'*. Surprisingly, Edward Lhuyd's achievements are barely recognised in Oswestry, whereas his wealthy ancestor, John Lloyd of Llanforda, is remembered as the builder of the Llwyd Mansion, the impressive black and white timber-framed building which still stands in the centre of the town.

In spite of the varied and excellent displays exhibited within the Heritage Centre, the best way to take in the 'feel' of Oswestry and its past is to walk the Town Trail which winds its way through medieval streets, past ancient buildings, sites and monuments. A visit on market day with its numerous street stalls becomes a special experience as the town draws in shoppers from Shropshire and mid Wales, together with farmers attending the Smithfield. On such days, Oswestry truly reflects its function as an ancient market town, retaining its strong ties with the agriculture of the hills and plains which surround it.

The B4580 Llansilin road out of Oswestry soon leaves the hustle and bustle of the town. A short distance out of town is a signpost to the 'Racecourse' which, now a local beauty spot, was once a popular venue for horse-racing, the last race being run here in 1850. The figure of eight circuit is about a mile and a half in length and on clear days, offers spectacular views of the surrounding countryside.

Within a few miles, the road crosses into Wales under the shelter of the gentle, wooded slopes of the Berwyn mountains. Just over the border is the small village of Rhyd-y-Croesau, situated on the river Cynllaith which acts as the border between Wales and England. The road continues through the valley of the Cynllaith and eventually arrives at Llansilin, the largest village in this remote, beautiful pastoral area, surrounded by rounded grassy hills. The focal point of the village is the parish church, dedicated to St Silin, an early missionary who also gave his name to the

Llwyd Mansion, Oswestry. [ES]

village. The church is built on the site of an early Celtic monastery or *clas* which was a centre of learning and culture. The thirteenth-century church was of cruciform design, with an aisled nave: the carvings on the east and west pillars of the arcade belong to this period. The fifteenth and sixteenth centuries brought changes, with the church becoming a rectangular building and a panelled ceiling and gallery being added at the west end. The present church boasts two equal bodies of four bays. The north aisle has a chapel dedicated to St Silin and used to contain a statue of him. Unfortunately, in 1646, during the time of the Civil War, Parliamentary troops took possession of the church and destroyed the statue, together with the fine east window and the figures in the rood loft. Above the south doors bullet holes can still be seen serving as a reminder that this tranquil valley was once exposed to violence and destruction.

In 1720, the old timber tower was burnt down and replaced in 1859 by the stone tower we see today. Between 1889 and 1890, major restoration work was carried out and the beautifully carved fourteenth century roof was restored and fully revealed. Fragments of a stone altar, buried beneath the church floor and decorated with three small crosses cut into the stone, were also revealed during these renovations. This now forms the window sill on the south side of the chancel. Displayed in a frame on the north wall are the brass plates of the old box pews which were removed during renovation. The timber was then used for the seats in the chancel. A close look at the north wall outside the church, reveals a line, running through the stonework, which was used by the villagers when they played the game of 'Fives' in the churchyard. On the south side of the church is the grave of Huw Morus, a renowned Cavalier poet, who lived in the neighbouring Ceiriog Valley. The large churchyard has many ancient yew trees which are reputed to be over 1,000 years old. Also situated in the church yard is the old National School which was built in 1823.

Little change has taken place in the layout of Llansilin over the centuries. As with many remote rural villages, it has been difficult to maintain the several shops and small industries that supported the village. Many of the shops are now private dwellings and, although farming is still very much a part of local life, other employment has now to be sought outside the village.

St Silin's Well was originally situated in the centre of a field. In 1882 the old well chamber was filled in and the water piped to a more central position in the village, opposite the church, where the water flows undisturbed.

The area surrounding the village shows evidence of prehistoric activity with many artefacts from the Stone, Bronze and Iron Ages being unearthed here. There are also numerous well-preserved, listed buildings in and around the village which reflect a richness of domestic architecture going back many centuries. As there are many streams in the area, there were also many water mills, some of which were working until well into the twentieth century.

Many footpaths radiate from Llansilin along which walkers and pony trekkers can explore this peaceful valley. For the more energetic visitor, the Gyrn, which dominates the village, offers a pleasant climb rising to 523 metres. A few years ago, Gyrn Moelfrewas featured in the film *The Englishman Who Went Up a Hill and Came Down a Mountain*, starring

Hugh Grant, which told the story of how the local inhabitants, so incensed that their mountain was not officially recognised as a mountain because of its lack of height, decided to add the necessary number of feet to it by hauling quantities of earth up its slopes until the official height was achieved. Filming in the area obviously brought in welcome revenue, plus the opportunity for many villagers to be extras in the film. It also advertised the beauty of the area to all who saw it.

Apart from its natural beauty and tranquil setting, Llansilin can proudly claim one of Wales' greatest heroes as its own, for a few miles south of the village, off the Llangedwyn Road, are the remains of Sycharth, reputed to be the birthplace of Owain Glyndŵr. Today all that remains is a grassy mound, but was originally, in all probability a Norman motte and bailey castle. Glyndŵr was descended from the princes of Powys and Deheubarth and spent most of his childhood years at Sycharth. There is no doubt that he enjoyed a comfortable and secure family life, some might say an affluent life-style, as the son of a man who wielded great power and authority in the Marcher regions. His father also held lands in Glyndyfrdwy in the Dee Valley, together with lands in south-west Wales which had belonged to his wife's family. To complete his education, Glyndŵr was sent to London where he was to study law at the Inns of Court. Then, as in the tradition of the times, as the son of landed gentry, he was educated at arms by the Lord of Oswestry, Richard Fitzalan. It is known that during this period he was a squire to Henry Bolingbroke, and served with distinction in the army of Richard II during the Scottish wars. On his return home to Sycharth he was regarded as a liberal-minded, brave and generous man, heir to large tracts of land in north, mid and south-west Wales. It seems that he maintained these characteristics, even when he later rebelled against the English king. Edmund Mortimer, a powerful Marcher Lord supportive of Glyndŵr, speaks the following in Shakespeare's, Henry IV, Part 1:

> *... he is a worthy gentleman,*
> *Exceedingly well-read, and profited*
> *In strange concealments, valiant as a lion*
> *And wondrous affable, and as bountiful*
> *As mines of India.*

After spending some time in Sycharth, Glyndŵr moved to Glyndyfrdwy from where he married Margaret, daughter of Sir David Hanmer, a Justice of the King's Bench in Hanmer, a detached portion of the old county of Flintshire known as Maelor Saesneg (English Maelor). Glyndŵr shared his time between Glyndyfrdwy and Sycharth which gave him and his family a very comfortable lifestyle. His contemporary, the bard Iolo Goch, was a frequent guest at Sycharth, and described it in an ode as a place of generous hospitality. The hall was surrounded by lush parkland, with a vineyard, orchards, a lake full of fish and a mill. In 1858, when George Borrow visited Sycharth on his travels through Wales, he sat down on the grassy hillock, all that remained of Glyndŵr mansion, and read an English translation that he had made of Iolo Goch's poem describing the splendour of the place in Owain's days. Borrow includes this translation in his book *Wild Wales*.

Glyndŵr's peaceful existence came to an abrupt end when Lord Grey of Ruthin seized some of his land. Fortunately, after seeking redress from the law, Glyndŵr was able to retrieve his land. This only further antagonised Lord Grey and, in his second attempt to annex Glyndŵr's land, he was supported by the king, Henry IV. Again Glyndŵr sought redress from the law but this was denied to him, and when one of his homes, possibly Sycharth, was attacked by Lord Grey, he raised his standard, the Red Dragon, and sought revenge on his attacker. He soon had an army of 4,000 followers and in the summer of 1400, attacked and destroyed the town of Ruthin. In September of that same year, Glyndŵr had himself proclaimed Prince of Wales and he went from victory to victory. Each triumph against the English king became a spur for independence.

Such was Glyndŵr's success that, in the summer of 1404, he summoned his followers to Machynlleth where he convened the first Welsh parliament. In order to strengthen his cause, he negotiated with France, at that time an enemy of England, and set about producing a blueprint for the future government of an independent Wales.

Despite proving himself to be an able statesman and a brave military leader, Glyndŵr's army was exhausted and his resources depleted, and his fortunes began to decline in 1405. King Henry IV was now determind to rid himself of Glyndŵr and gain control of the territories west of Offa's

Dyke and the tide turned against the Welsh prince. His wife and children, apart from one son, were captured and Glyndŵr himself fled to the security of the Welsh mountains, becoming a fugitive. He was later declared an outlaw by Henry IV. In 1415, the English king, Henry V, offered Glyndŵr a pardon, but the response was as silent as his native mountains. There is no certainty as to where Glyndŵr ended his days. Some say that he spent them at the home of his daughter in the Golden Valley in Herefordshire whereas others say that he became a priest. The popular legend amongst many in Wales is that Glyndŵr and his companions are not dead, but sleeping in a cave, deep in the mountains of Snowdonia, ready to rise again and save Wales. As one stands in the green, lush, peaceful valley of the Cynllaith, surveying what remains of Sycharth, it is hard to believe that such a place nurtured a man who changed the face of Welsh history. Whatever has been written about Glyndŵr over the centuries, there is no doubt that he was, in the words of the distinguished English historian G. M. Trevalyan: 'This wonderful man, an attractive and unique figure in a period of debased and selfish politics, actually revived for a few years the virtual independence of a great part of his country.'

From Sycharth, returning to Llansilin, the B4580 road winds it way to the village of Llanrhaeadr-ym-Mochnant and on to Pistyll Rhaeadr. It is possible to either drive or walk up to the waterfall. In the far corner of the village is a sign – 'I'r Rhaeadr' (To the Waterfall) and from here the narrow road meanders through a quiet, steep-sided valley, hugging the banks of the river. If driving, the motorist must be aware of the narrowness of the road and that passing places are few and far between. Walkers can follow a footpath along the river bank which acts as the boundary between Wrexham County Borough and the county of Powys. The distance from the village to the falls is approximately three miles. At the head of the valley, the road peters out into a car park besides Tan-y-Pistyll, a cottage-style building which is also a café. From here, a short walk will bring one suddenly to a spectacular view of the river Disgynfa, a small river which rises high up in the Berwyn mountains, plunging over the edge of a steep cliff from a height of seventy-three metres. Surrounded by a natural, rocky amphitheatre that has been gorged by the elements over thousands of years, the waterfall seems to fall from the sky. The highest waterfall in

Wales, it is also claimed to be the highest south of the Scottish Highlands. It is actually higher than the Niagra Falls in North America.

To get a closer look, follow the path which leads to a bridge from where the water can be seen to fall in an unbroken torrent to unknown depths. It then spurts out through a cleft in the rocks to fall further and cascade over the black boulders, glistening wet in the spray. When George Borrow took his first glimpse of Pistyll Rhaeadr, he recorded that he saw the waterfall as '... an immense skein of silk agitated and disturbed by tempestuous blasts, or to the long tail of a gray courser at furious speed.' Others, on first seeing the waterfall, have thought that the water, at certain points, seems to be frozen still. But this illusion is broken in seconds by the sound of the turbulence at the base of the falls, reminding the viewer that this is indeed 'living water'. Is it any wonder that Pistyll Rhaeadr has attracted so many visitors?

Above the falls is Moel Sych, the highest of the Berwyn Mountains at 827 metres. Further along the ridge comes Cadair Berwyn and Cadair Bronwen. Nestling below the crags of Moel Sych is an isolated lake, Llyn Lluncaws. A challenging hill walk up to this lake commences from the road below the Tan-y-Pistyll car parks. The grassy track leads up through the bracken-covered slopes and, after a steep climb, levels out onto upland moors with the lake, on a still, bright sunny day, reflecting the rugged outline of the Berwyn Ridge. Literally translated into English, Llyn Lluncaws becomes the 'Lake of a Picture of a Cheese'! Many have submitted a variety of reasons for such an unusual name. One suggestion is that the shape of the lake is almost circular, similar to the shape of a cheese. Another suggests that at night, when the moon is full, its reflection in the still waters of the lake again appears like a round of yellow cheese against the darkness. But the magnificence of the rocky amphitheatre in which the lake lies has supplied another explanation for the lake's name. Not far from the lake is an ancient trackway – Ffordd Gam Elen (Helen's Crooked Road) – Helen being a Welsh princess said to have married the Roman Emperor Maximus. According to the legend, Helen was leading her legions across the Berwyns and rested on the slopes of Moel Sych above the lake. As Helen attempted to unload provisions for her men, she unfortunately dropped one of the cheeses meant to sustain them and it rolled down the mountainside and into the

Pistyll Rhaeadr. [WAW]

lake. Since that day to this, the lake has been known as Llyn Lluncaws!

Although not regarded by some hill walkers and climbers as 'true mountains' when compared to those of Snowdonia, the Berwyn Mountains have their own particular challenges such as boggy ground, knee-high heather, sudden steep ascents and no clear paths to the summits of Moel Sych, Cadair y Berwyn and Cadair Bronwen. Many people who visit the villages in the valleys below are unaware that the Berwyns exist, as very few roads penetrate the mountains. The roads are often only single tracks with very few passing places, as a result of which the Berwyns remain in splendid isolation and have not suffered the problems of erosion seen in many of the more popular mountain areas of north Wales. The name 'Berwyn' is said to be that of a mythical giant who lived on the mountain named Cadair-y-Berwyn (Berwyn's Chair). The neighbouring peak of Cadair Bronwen takes its name from the Welsh chronicles of *The Mabinogion*, Bronwen being the name of a princess featured in the chronicles. Below these two peaks is the smaller peak of Carnedd y Ci (The Hill of the Dog) named, according to legend, after the dogs from Hell which are said to roam the area. Perhaps this legend is a reminder to those who walk these mountains of the hazardous conditions which can result when an enjoyable climb suddenly becoming a challenge to one's fitness and hill-craft. Between Cadair-y-Berwyn and Cadair Bronwen is Bwlch Maen Gwynedd at 731 metres, one of the two longest passes in Wales. It is said that Owain Gwynedd summoned the greatest force that Wales had yet raised to meet the advancing army of Henry II on his march from Shrewsbury in 1169. The wild landscape and ever-changing weather, plus the unity of all the Welsh princes proved too much for Henry's army and his advance into Wales was halted in a battle which took place in the Ceiriog Valley.

Not only do the Berwyns give us a variety of walking experiences, a place of great solitude, remote from the stresses and strains of the twenty-first century, they also gives us an expanse of landscape with reminders of our past such as ring cairns, platform houses and old sheep folds, visual evidence that people once lived in this high, remote area. Because of the diversity of plant and wild life to be found on these rolling hills and heather moorlands, the area is now under the protection of the Countryside Council for Wales and the Game Conservancy Trust and a

National Nature Reserve has also been created. A visit to Pistyll Rhaeadr not only gives us an opportunity to share with past travellers the wonder of this natural phenomenon, but also acts as a stimulus to explore further this little known landscape of mountains, rolling hills and remote villages.

The village of Llanrhaeadr-ym-Mochnant sits snugly on the eastern slopes of the Berwyns. Despite its isolation, it continues to attract visitors en route to the waterfall, and walkers exploring the varied landscape on offer. Some, however, particularly those interested in Welsh history, may be visiting the village in order to familiarise themselves with the place where Bishop William Morgan worked on his translation of the Bible into Welsh during his time as a vicar here (1578–88). Morgan was born in 1545 in Tŷ Mawr Wybrnant, in the parish of Penmachno, a secluded valley near Betws-y-Coed. It is said that he received his early education from a monk and completed his later education at Cambridge. He was vicar in numerous north- and mid-Wales parishes before coming to Llanrhaeadr. Permission had been given by Queen Elizabeth I that the Welsh language could be used within the Church and in 1563, an act of parliament was passed demanding that the Welsh bishops provide a translation into Welsh of not only the Book of Common Prayer but also the Bible. Prior to this, Elizabeth's father, Henry VIII, had banned the use of the Welsh language in churches. Some translations of the New Testament and the Book of Common Prayer had been completed by William Salesbury, an Oxford educated literary lawyer in 1567. Salesbury had a deep love of the Welsh language and was afraid that its very existence was severely threatened. Having completed his initial work, with the help and support of two colleagues, Salesbury fully intended to translate the Old Testament but he published nothing after 1567 and died in 1584. It fell to the determination and Welsh-language skills of William Morgan to complete the first full translation of the Bible into Welsh, which was in those days a mammoth task. Despite numerous altercations with some of his quarrelsome parishioners which interrupted his work, he had the staunch support of many. The work was finally published in 1588 and there is no doubt that, at a time when the Welsh language was in danger of disappearing, the publication was an event of crucial importance to the survival of the language. In 1595, William Morgan became bishop of

Llanrhaeadr-ym-Mochnant. [ES]

Llandaff in south Wales, but was moved up to north Wales to become bishop of St Asaph in 1601. During this period, he revised his translation and published a new edition of the Book of Common Prayer and also completed a new version of the New Testament. He died in 1604. The vicarage where William Morgan completed his great work stands in a quiet corner of Llanrhaeadr not far from the church. Access into the vicarage is possible through prior arrangement with the present owners.

The church, dedicated to St Dogfan, stands on the site of a *clas* or Celtic monastery. Inside, it shows signs of much restoration with little evidence of the original building to be seen. What it does reveal, however, is a Celtic wheel cross which is unusual in its design and is said to be the only one of its kind in Wales. Similar patterns and carvings have been found on crosses and standing stones in Scotland and the Isle of Man where they are very common. What is the connection one wonders? According to many historians the Celtic tribes moved from place to place as new invaders moved in. It is possible that a particular tribe settled here in this remote valley with its natural defence of hills and mountains, bringing their distinctive stone-carving patterns with them.

Leaving the tranquility of Llanrhaeadr-ym-Mochnant on the road sign-posted 'Llanarmon Dyffryn Ceiriog' the landscape soon changes with the lower slopes of the Berwyns gradually rising up from the valley floor below. These lower slopes are dotted with isolated farmhouses, their pasture land soon giving way to moorland. The narrow road reaches its highest point at 421 metres and on a clear day, the view is quite spectacular with bare mountain tops acting as a dramatic backdrop to the heather-clad moors.

Gradually, the road drops down into the Ceiriog valley and the village of Llanarmon Dyffryn Ceiriog (Llanarmon DC) situated at its head. The river Ceiriog, which rises high above the village in the Berwyn mountains, flows swiftly through the village on its journey down the valley, eventually flowing into the more sedate waters of the River Dee. The village sits neatly around a small square surrounded by green meadows, wooded slopes and high moorland. In the past, the village had numerous shops, a smithy, a mill, a post office and a variety of cottage industries as well as a church, chapels and a school. It was also a busy stopping off point for drovers driving their livestock from the Welsh hinterland over the mountains to be sold in England. Today only the school, the church and a few chapels survive, with fewer working farms.

St Dogfan's Church, Llanrhaeadr-yn-Mochnant. [ES]

As with many similar villages, tourism has been encouraged as an alternative. With its varied landscape, the village can offer a variety of activities for those who 'want to get away from it all.' These include walking, pony-trekking, fishing and mountain-biking. Situated in the village square are two excellent hotels which cater for these activities.

Overlooking the village is the church dedicated to St Garmon, a French travelling saint who set up the first Christian settlement here in the fifth century. The church steeple rises above ancient yew trees reputed to be over 1,000 years old. The present church was rebuilt in 1846 on the site of an older building. Inside, it has the unusual feature of having two pulpits, one on the right-hand side and one on the left. It is said that the Roman Catholics of the village shared the church with the Protestant congregation during the eighteenth century, their services taking place at different times. The left-hand pulpit would have been used during Catholic worship and the right-hand pulpit for the Protestant worship, this being the only pulpit used in present-day services. An interesting link to this past oddity of Catholics and Protestants sharing the same building for their worship, all be it at different times, is the confession box now to be seen in the West Arms Hotel. Was this once a feature of the church's interior and removed when the Catholics no longer worshipped there? No one, it seems, can confirm this. As one passes out of the circular churchyard, a grassy mound rises up just inside the gate. This is said to be a 'Preaching Mound' which pre-dates any building in the village.

Surprisingly, Llanarmon Dyffryn Ceiriog still remains relatively undiscovered. In spite of its close proximity to the English border and the A5, one of the main tourist routes into north Wales, the village and a greater part of the valley have managed to retain their cultural heritage and unspoilt countryside. On a hillside just outside the village is the home of one of Wales' best loved lyric poets, John Ceiriog Hughes, who was born in Pen-y-Bryn farm in 1832 and named after the river which ran below his home. Although he spent much of his adult life away from Llanarmon, his poems reflect his love of nature and the countryside nurtured during his childhood which was spent in this valley. He had the ability to blend words and create 'word-pictures' of places that were familiar to him. Many of his poems have been set to music and are still sung in concerts and *eisteddfodau* throughout Wales. To many Welsh people, whether they live in Wales or in other countries, their first memory of hearing or learning a Welsh poem as a child would probably be one written by Ceiriog.

Leaving Llanarmon Dyffryn Ceiriog, it is difficult to believe that in 1923, Parliament was asked to consider a proposal by the Warrington Corporation for the creation of two large reservoirs within the valley. The plan was to acquire 13,600 acres, evict the local population and drown the villages of Llanarmon, Tregeiriog and Pentre. Fortunately, a groundswell of opposition rose up against these proposals with Prime Minister David Lloyd George condemning and rejecting the whole project after paying a visit to the valley. Had Lloyd George not spoken so passionately in its defence, describing the valley as 'A little bit of heaven on earth' and asking, 'Why should anyone want to flood this exquisite little valley?' its beauty might have disappeared forever.

The B4500 road leaves the village of Llanarmon Dyffryn Ceiriog running more or less side-by-side with the river Ceiriog down the valley. About two miles down the road is the small hamlet of Tregeiriog. Once a bustling valley community with a school, chapels, shops, a mill and a cheese factory, plus a nearby quarry providing alternative work to farming the land, it contributed to the rich heritage and culture of the valley. Although farming is still very much a part of village life, tourism is becoming the major employer. Tregeiriog has also nurtured another well-known Welsh poet. Long before Ceiriog was born, Huw Morus (1622–1709) lived in Pont-y-Meibion, a farm a little further down the valley. He is perhaps better known by his bardic name *Eos Ceiriog* (the Ceiriog nightingale). An ardent royalist living in the time of Cromwell, he is remembered for his political poems, attacking the parliamentarians in his verse. He did this in such a way that his words were not seen to be openly condemning, thus saving him from the persecution suffered by other critics of his time. He is also remembered in the valley for the many *carolau* (carols) he wrote particularly those relating to the *Plygain*, an early morning religious service held on Christmas Day in many churches in Wales. These *carolau* are still sung in the valley and in neighbouring valleys where the *Plygain* is still commemorated. Many of his poems were written out of doors where he sat in a special chair. This chair can be seen today in nearby Erw Gerrig farm where his brother lived and a memorial to him stands at Pont-y-Meibion Farm.

A short distance down the valley is the hamlet of Pandy which is named after the fulling mill, now the public house known as the 'Woolpack'. According to records, this may have been the first mill of its kind transforming local woven woollen material into flannel using 'fullers earth'. Here at Pandy it is also possible to walk along the track of the Glyn Valley Tramway constructed in 1873 to service, primarily, the many quarries in the valley. It became an important lifeline for the valley communities with the outside world, taking out the mineral wealth of the valley and bringing in coal, building materials, agricultural goods and a variety of commodities for the inns and shops. The tramway was extended up to Hendre quarry between Tregeiriog and Pandy in 1888. High above Pandy is Pandy Crag, which has been identified as a possible Regionally Important Geological Site. Pandy Crag and surrounding area have a great variety of mineral deposits, many having been quarried in the past. Many caves are situated along the valley road which, although now flooded, can be viewed through an iron gate. George Borrow on his visit to the valley in 1854 described it as: '... wild and solitary to an extraordinary degree, the brook or torrent running in the middle of it, covered with alder tree.'

Continuing down the valley, Glynceiriog is the largest of the valley settlements. Sometimes referred to by its Welsh name – Llansantffraid Glynceiriog – it is affectionately referred to by the inhabitants as just 'Glyn'. For many years, it was dominated by the slate quarries perched on the slopes just above the village. Prior to this, it was largely a farming community with sheep being the chief source of income. The women of the community would spin and weave the wool resulting in a flourishing cottage industry. Later, two flannel mills were built to develop this industry further. Slate quarrying had been a major industry in the valley for several hundred years with records showing that roofing slates from the valley were used at nearby Chirk Castle in 1529. With the opening of *Chwarel Wynne* in 1750, and the increasing demand for slate, the quarry supported a large workforce from Glynceiriog and the other valley villages. Unfortunately, as the demand for slate deteriorated the quarry closed down. In recent years attempts have been made to create a museum displaying the history of slate quarrying in the valley with guided walks through the caverns where the quarry men faced dangers on a daily basis, long before the days of Health and Safety regulations. Nearby is a nature trail wandering through woodland, home to a variety of flora and fauna.

The Ceiriog Valley has been a vibrant centre of Christianity for well over 1,600 years since Celtic saints first sought peace and solitude in this secluded place. The close-knit community of Glynceiriog was deeply religious and almost exclusively Welsh-speaking, despite its close proximity to the English border. During the eighteenth century, when Nonconformity swept through the valley, it was said that the fervour of worship in the Glynceiriog area was particularly intense. This is reflected in the numerous chapels and churches to be seen in the village today. A short distance from the High Street is the Ceiriog Memorial Institute built in 1911 to commemorate notable Welsh people from the valley, in particular the valley poets already mentioned. It is still in use today and open to visitors. On the outskirts of the village is the parish church dedicated to St Ffraid (Bridget), a Celtic saint. Situated on a hillside, it has a panoramic view of the village and surrounding valley. The earliest remnants of the church, which date from *c*.1100, can be seen in the lower part of the tower when the church was a *'capella'* attached to Llangollen church. By 1250, both churches had become linked to the Cistercian monastery at Valle Crucis, an association which continued until the dissolution of the monastery by Henry VIII in 1536. As the road leads out of Glynceiriog, the wooded slopes of the valley become more lush with the river Ceiriog continuing on its way through green meadows.

The road eventually comes to the tiny village of Pontfadog, which sits virtually on the banks of the river. Here the Tramway Waiting Room of the former Glyn Valley Tramway is well worth a visit as it houses details and photographs of the tramway which played such an important part in the life of the valley between 1873 and 1935, serving the quarries, the mines, the mills and the valley villages by providing a passenger service. Nowadays, the valley does not echo to the sound of wagons rolling down the tramway, or the hooter summoning the quarrymen to work. Only the sounds of sheep and cattle vie with the call of the buzzard circling high above the valley floor.

According to *Brut y Tywysogion* (The Chronicle of the Princes) the battle of Crogen was fought in the Ceiriog Valley in 1165 between the independent Welsh princes, under the leadership of Owain Gwynedd, against the forces of Henry II. The English forces suffered heavy losses and eventual defeat, due to the fact that they were unused to fighting in this type of terrain and their long march from Shrewsbury had taken its toll. This battle is reputed to have taken place near Pontfadog, where a number of farms named after the battle – Crogen Wladys, Crogen Iddon and Plas Crogen – tend to support this claim. Others, however, claim the battle took place higher up the valley near Tregeiriog. Whichever claim is correct, there is no doubt that the valley, guarded and sheltered by the Berwyn Mountains, was an ideal environment in which the Welsh could resist the invasions from over Offa's Dyke.

Sitting on the hillside above Pontfadog is an unusual house, its style reminiscent of the type of houses built in the foothills of India. It was the home of Sir Vyner Brook, the White Rajah of Sarawak.

On leaving Pontfadog, the road twists and turns alongside the river Ceiriog with trees on either side forming an archway of greenery. Soon Castle Mill appears on the left, the site of an early Norman fortress and in fact the road crosses the ancient Offa's Dyke at this point with England on the other side of the River Ceiriog. A flourishing trout farm soon comes into view and nearby a road on the right signposted to Weston Rhyn goes over the old stone bridge, Pont Faen, into Shropshire. This is the oldest bridge in the valley, which at one time carried the Chester–Cardiff road.

From Pont Faen there is a good view to be had of the Chirk aqueduct and viaduct. A closer look at these two magnificent constructions can be had a little further on by parking in Station Road, a short distance along the valley road on the left. Crossing the valley road you will come to a gateway which leads down a steep, wooded path to a spot below the two massive structures. Their height is quite overwhelming, their graceful arches rising it seems to the clouds.

The aqueduct, which is seventy-feet high, was built between 1796 and 1801 by Thomas Telford and William Jessop to carry the Ellesmere Canal. The trough carrying the canal water is made of iron plates bolted together with side walls of stone quarried from nearby Pont Faen. With the

Chirk aquaduct and viaduct. [ES]

development of rail travel Henry Robertson, a Scottish engineer, erected the viaduct between 1846–8, rebuilding it in 1858. The 30.5 metre-high stone structure carried the Shrewsbury & Chester Railway. It stands some thirty feet above the adjoining aqueduct. For those who have a good head for heights, a more spectacular walk can be achieved by following the tow path which runs along the canalside, across the aqueduct. From this vantage point, magnificent views open up, the Ceiriog valley ahead with Chirk Castle rising above Castle Woods to the right and the river Ceiriog nearing the end of its journey, far below.

The name 'Chirk' is thought by some to be an English corruption of the name of the river Ceiriog, others have suggested that it is the dialect form of the word 'kirk' or 'church'. The town's Welsh name – *'Y Waun'* meaning meadow or moorland – is possibly derived from the fact that the original hamlet that established itself on a hill overlooking the border of Wales and England, was surrounded by lush meadows and bleak moorland. Whether we refer to it as 'Chirk' or 'Y Waun', there is no doubt that its strategic position was important, not only to the native Welsh but to the invading English. Records show that Chirk and the surrounding area have been influenced over the centuries by the Celts, the Romans, the Welsh, the Normans and the English. As the Norman occupation expanded along the borders, they strengthened their position by building motte and bailey castles. The first castle at Chirk was of this type, and remains of its motte can still be seen in the shape of a conical mound to the rear of 'The Mount', a three-storey Georgian building situated on the corner of Church Street opposite the church. From this position, the crossing point of the river Ceiriog below could be easily observed and guarded. Up until 1282, Chirk was within the Lordship of Chirkland, with one Llywelyn ap Gruffydd ap Madog as its lord. Once described by a contemporary poet as 'the dragon of Chirk with the obstinate spear', he was no doubt a troublemaker and an enemy in the eyes of the English king, Edward I. In June 1282, Llywelyn's lands were forfeited to the Crown and handed over to Roger Mortimer and a new marcher lordship was created, known as the Marcher Lordship of Chirkland. Although becoming an English stronghold, it always remained in Wales.

At the request of his king, Roger Mortimer began building a much larger, stronger castle in Chirk. Work probably started in the late 1290s and tradition has it that it was completed by 1310, but it could have been later. Many see the castle's design as reminiscent of Beaumaris castle in Anglesey with its imposing towers at four corners. There is no doubt that Edward I saw Chirk Castle as a vital part of his 'Ring of Stone', the term he used to describe the castles he built in north Wales in order to control the native population. Over the years, the castle played a prominent part in keeping an English presence on this Welsh borderland. In 1595, it was bought by the Myddleton family for £5,000. The Myddletons claimed descent from Ririd Flaidd (Ririd the Wolf) who possessed lordships in Meirionydd, and the family arms have a wolf's head motif. The castle has remained in the ownership of the Myddleton family for over three and a half centuries. In 1981, it was conveyed to the National Trust with members of the Myddleton family continuing to live there. Regarded today as one of the great historic houses of Britain, surrounded by extensive parkland and impressive gardens, the castle strikes an imposing image, its massive stone walls and towers giving an impression of great strength. Within the parkland are numerous walks with Offa's Dyke running north to south across the grounds. The castle provides not only a step back into history but offers a variety of cultural and educational programmes for the many visitors, both local and tourists, to enjoy.

On leaving the castle grounds, one's attention is drawn to magnificent ornamental gates, the work of the Davies brothers, who lived and worked from their smithy at Croesfoel on the outskirts of Wrexham. Commissioned in 1712, the gates bear the Myddleton family arms and are made up of intricately designed panels of wrought-iron work. Other examples of the Davies brothers' skills can be seen throughout north-east Wales.

The town of Chirk is situated on the old turnpike road from London to Holyhead, along which stagecoaches carried the Irish mail. Now known as the B5020, it was formerly the A5, the famous historic route created by the great nineteenth-century engineer Thomas Telford. The town possesses a clutch of fine houses which reflect its past prosperity gained from the coalmining industry and ironworks which played a major part in Chirk's social history from the sixteenth to the twentieth century.

The parish church, dedicated to St Mary, has a prominent position in

Chirk Castle gates. [ES]

Chirk Castle. [GAJ]

the town, with some Norman remnants of the original church dating from the twelfth century still evident. Over the centuries, numerous repairs and alterations have taken place, but this does not impair its overall appearance. Inside are many monuments to the Myddleton family of Chirk Castle and the Trevor family of nearby Brynkinallt Hall (one member of which was the mother of the Duke of Wellington). At the rear of the churchyard is a highly decorative small building, a mausoleum built in 1904 for the five-year-old daughter of the second Lord Trevor. Based on a Norman-style church, the architecture shows a variety of features typical of the Norman period.

Situated on the main street of the town is the Hand Hotel, an early nineteenth century building with later additions. It served as a coaching inn on Telford's London to Holyhead road, and continues to meet the needs of the modern-day traveller. Above the entrance to the hotel hangs the hotel sign – the red hand which appears as a heraldic device on the Myddleton family's arms. There are numerous local legends or myths which attempt to explain the origin of the red hand or 'Bloody hand of Chirk'. One legend is said to arise from a dispute which arose between two members of the family as to who should inherit the castle. A race between the two contenders was arranged, the first to reach and touch the castle gates to be acclaimed the winner. Unfortunately, the first to reach the gate at the finishing line was deprived of his victory by a supporter of his rival who drew his sword and cut off his hand before he was able to touch the gate. Another legend has it that the red hand is a curse upon the Myddleton family and will only be removed if a prisoner survived ten years imprisonment in the castle dungeon! A final story tells of an early member of the Myddleton family being severely injured in battle; he placed his blood-covered hand on his white tunic leaving a bloody imprint which then became his heraldic symbol. The reality is much more straight-forward. The red hand is the symbol of Ulster in Ireland and when James I introduced the title of baronet to help pay for a military campaign there, all the newly-formed baronets were entitled to have the Red Hand of Ulster as part of their heraldic arms.

A new section of the A5 has been constructed to by-pass Chirk in recent years thus relieving the town of ever-increasing volumes of modern traffic. Today, Chirk continues to provide a welcome to visitors and tourists, a convenient centre from which to explore and experience a

The London–Holyhead road at Chirk. The War Memorial on the right was designed by Eric Gill [WAW]

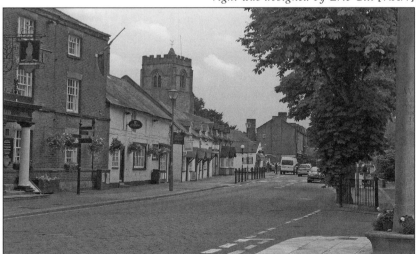

variety of interesting things to see and do, be they historical buildings and structures, walking and exploring the Berwyn mountains or cruising the Llangollen Canal.

Wonder 2

Froncysyllte – LLANGOLLEN BRIDGE – Llangollen Town – Plas Newydd - Canal & Horseshoe Falls – Valle Crucis Abbey – Dinas Brân – Ruabon – Rhosllannerchrugog.

ON LEAVING CHIRK, travelling westwards towards Llangollen, new industries which have replaced the old, present a contrasting picture against a green and wooded backdrop of gentle hills. Soon the road links up with the A5 and again one wonders at the genius of Thomas Telford's achievemnent in constructing this route. The road now progresses above the Dee and very soon arrives at the village of Froncysyllte clinging to the hillside above the valley. Today, its cluster of houses, church and inns are witnesses to a constant flow of traffic transporting tourists through the beautiful Vale of Llangollen. The village was once dependent on the nearby quarry which, when working to full capacity, produced limestone which was transported down a series of tramways to the village where the stone was crushed. A further series of tramways carried the crushed lime to the Trevor Basin on the other side of the Dee Valley, which was, during the early nineteenth century, a busy wharf and an important transport centre for the Llangollen Canal. The limestone would then be transported along the canal system as far as the Midlands where it would be used in the process of iron-smelting. This journey was only made possible because of the remarkable aqueduct, designed and built by Thomas Telford between 1795 and 1805. Considered to be one of Telford's masterpieces, it carries the canal 126 feet above the river Dee in an iron trough over 1,000 feet long, supported by eighteen hollow, stone pillars. Sir Walter Scott described it as the greatest work of art he had ever seen.

The road bridge and aqueduct at Froncysyllte. [WAW]

On the day the aqueduct was opened, it is said that 8,000 people were present to see a flotilla of barges sailing across a narrow stretch of water described by some as 'the stream in the sky' and by others watching from the valley below, as 'ships in the sky'. In 2009, Pontcysyllte Aqueduct was made a UNESCO World Heritage Site. William Hazlitt, the renowned essayist, walking in this area on his way to Llangollen, stopped to look out over the view of Trevor, Froncysyllte and Pontcysyllte and described what he saw as a 'Roman amphitheatre of hills'. In spite of industrial developments the view is still a splendid introduction to the delightful landscape of the Vale of Llangollen which lies ahead.

As the A5 leaves Froncysyllte, its wooded slopes give glimpses of the valley until it eventually opens out completely and the river Dee and the Llangollen Canal can be seen winding their way towards Llangollen. The opposite side of the valley boasts one of the finest carboniferous limestone escarpments in Britain and is now an area of Special Scientific Interest. Above the escarpment, the limestone plateau has revealed many traces of Early Bronze Age occupation, including cairns, barrows, circles and a standing stone. To the south of the valley, the gentle slopes of the northern edges of the Berwyns rise up above the A5. Ahead, Dinas Brân an isolated, steep hill rises up above the valley with the ruins of its castle silhouetted against the skyline.

Soon the road enters the town of Llangollen which is surrounded by the wooded slopes of hills and mountains and the site of another of the seven wonders of Wales – Llangollen Bridge – which has been the main crossing point of the river Dee since the thirteenth century in the form of a packhorse bridge. Tradition has it that John Trevor, bishop of St Asaph and chancellor of Chester, built a new, larger bridge in 1346. The present structure probably dates from around 1500, with its four unequal pointed arches. Due to the construction of the railway, a further arch was added in 1861 and the whole structure was widened in 1873. As the volume of traffic increased, the bridge underwent further widening in 1968–9 but, despite these changes, remains a handsome structure. When the travel writer H. V. Morton visited Llangollen in the early 1930s, he recorded in his book *In Search of Wales*: 'I could lean for hours over Bishop Trevor's bridge, admiring the dark pools, the sudden eddies, the quick shallow channels of the nut-brown Dee. It is a great thing for a town to have a salmon river whispering at its walls day and night …' The bridge remains a popular focal point for the town and no matter what season, continues to attract many visitors to enjoy the views from its parapet.

Llangollen is named after St Collen, a Celtic saint who, according to local legend, lived in a cave in the nearby Berwyn mountains during the late sixth and early seventh centuries. He is said to have been tempted by the *tylwyth teg* (fairies) to give up his simple life in exchange for a life of luxury, music and beautiful clothes. Collen resolutely shunned these temptations and continued his life of worship and prayer. Because of this link with St Collen, the town of Llangollen can be said to be a product of late Romano-British period, in existence before the Anglo-Saxon assault on Wales. Archaeological finds confirm the existence of early settlements on the uplands on either side of the valley and one can assume that the valley floor with its river and lush meadows encouraged alternative settlements. As it became more populated, Llangollen became a busy centre in the valley and many mills were built along the river bank both

Llangollen Bridge. [WAW]

up and down stream, with their water wheels set in such a way that they utilised the fast flowing waters of the river to advantage. One of the mills is situated close to the old bridge, although it no longer grinds corn, its building has survived and in recent years has undergone an impressive renovation, incorporating its wheel and shafts, into a pub-restaurant with a good reputation for serving appetising meals in an interesting and attractive environment.

Records indicate that this mill is the oldest mill building in Llangollen. Other mill buildings along the river have either become derelict or have been taken over as premises for other industries. For example, Mile End Mill, situated on the A5 not far from the Wild Pheasant Hotel, is now a canoeing centre which reflects the fact that the river provides ideal conditions for this ever-popular activity which brings many enthusiasts to the town. Two other mills at the other end of the town, across the bridge, namely Upper Dee Mill and Lower Dee Mill have provided alternative employment when the flannel weaving industry deteriorated. Upper Dee Mill situated opposite the Sarah Ponsonby Inn, together with Lower Dee Mill on the other side of the road, became the largest seed factory in Europe. Eventually some of the buildings of Upper Dee Mill were demolished and the land given over to housing. The remaining buildings became business units, but now its future is once again uncertain. Lower Dee Mill became a tourist attraction, housing the 'Doctor Who Experience' but this building has now disappeared and has been used for a development of riverside apartments.

There is no doubt that, over the centuries, Llangollen has become a haunt for travellers and tourists, particularly since the late eighteenth century when the town was visited by several famous writers such as John Ruskin, who described the town as: '… one of the most beautiful and delightful in Wales or anywhere else.' George Borrow the nineteenth-century writer and traveller stayed in Llangollen for several months whilst he explored the surrounding area on foot and recorded his exploits in his book *Wild Wales*, probably the best selling travelogue ever published about Wales. By this time, Llangollen had become a bustling market town, its canal used to transport slate from nearby quarries and its close proximity to the A5 route made it a popular coach halt for travellers using the London – Holyhead turnpike road. As a result of this, the town boasts many hostelries. Situated near the bridge is the Royal Hotel. Originally known as the King's Head, it changed its name after Queen Victoria, then a princess, stayed there in 1832. Not far from the Royal, is the Wynnstay Arms and further along, overlooking the river is the Hand Hotel, regarded in the nineteenth century as one of the principal coaching inns, with stables and servants ready to provide service and comfort for weary travellers. It is probable that the old town was centred around the Hand Hotel and the nearby Parish Church. It would have been a busy area with malt kilns and breweries, a timber yard and a fulling mill across the river, bakehouses and a variety of shops serving the terraced houses which lined the narrow streets.

A pathway leads from the Hand Hotel to the town's parish church which is dedicated to St Collen. It is known that other churches in the district were dedicated to the same saint but, after the Norman Conquest, there was a more definite interest and growing veneration for the Virgin Mary and most of the neighbouring churches adopted Mary as their patron instead. The original church dates from the thirteenth century and would have been much smaller than the church we see today, which has

Above: The Ladies of Llangollen. [WAW]

Right: The triangular memorial stone of the Ladies in Llangollen churchyard. [WAW]

been enlarged and restored in the eighteenth century so that it is now a fine example of a double-aisled church with a classical west tower. The interior of the church has much to interest the visitor, the most striking feature being the fine medieval hammer-beam roof with its elaborate oak carvings. A new lighting system was installed in 1967 which can be switched on by visitors thus enabling them to have a much closer study of the roof detail. The carvings range from the Madonna and Child to angels, creatures, birds and humans. Possibly the most unusual group of carvings can be seen above the archway, near the pulpit, which depicts firstly a man attempting to roll two barrels, one on top of the other. Next we see the man presumably enjoying the contents of the barrel and then, finally, we see him inside the barrel obviously determined to enjoy the contents to the last drop. Is it possible the carvers were using a local character known for his drinking habits as a model? Another medieval feature is the north door with its 'peep-holes' reminding us of the days when offenders could claim sanctuary in the church, a privilege which ceased in 1634. The south doorway dates from the twelfth century whilst a fourteenth-century tomb recess can also be found displaying original mouldings and carvings. A more recent, yet striking memorial, is the one situated in the south aisle to the 'Ladies of Llangollen ' whose presence in the town in the late eighteenth and early nineteenth centuries was the subject of much gossip and continues to fascinate visitors today.

On leaving the church, a painting in the porch records the structure of the church before the extension of 1863, it also has an interesting example of a churchwardens' chest, dated 1748, which has three keyholes. The reason for this oddity was because the parish was made of three districts at that time – Llan, Trevor and Glyn, each electing its own warden. All three wardens had to be present when the churchwardens' chest was unlocked, each warden having his own key. Moving through the churchyard one can not help but notice the triangular Gothic tombstone of the 'Ladies of Llangollen' together with their trusted housekeeper, Mary Carryll. Their story is fascinating, firstly because of their eccentricity and secondly, their life-style was such that it was questioned by many. Nevertheless they lived in Llangollen for over fifty years and contributed much to the society and culture of the town.

The 'Ladies' set up their home in 1780 at Plas Newydd which is situated on Butler Hill, on the outskirts of the town. Before settling in Llangollen, the 'Ladies', that is Lady Eleanor Butler and the Honourable Sarah Ponsonby, had developed a strong bond of friendship whilst living in Ireland. Although Eleanor was sixteen years older than Sarah, they both shared similar ideas, the most important being that they should be free to love and not be involved with any man. This was very much against the wishes of both their families, who expected them to accept offers of marriage. In order to escape from this, they plotted to flee from Ireland by ship to England. Unfortunately, the plan failed and they were returned to their respective families who made great efforts to end their relationship. Despite strong opposition this strange friendship survived and ultimately, their families relented and, accompanied by Mary Carryll, they left Ireland in 1778, unaware that they would never return. Arriving near Milford Haven, they visited many places of interest before making their way north, eventually arriving in Llangollen, described in Eleanor's journal as, 'a pretty village on the River Dee.' (Elizabeth Mavor, *The Ladies of Llangollen*, Michael Joseph,1971). It took them some time to find a suitable home, but they eventually found a cottage in the secluded Pengwern Valley. They renamed the cottage 'Plas Newydd' and spent the early days in precious isolation setting out plans to alter their home and garden, involving themselves in a variety of other creative activities and taking long walks. Although bound by financial constraints, they were able to complete extravagant alterations to their home and garden and what we see today is what they achieved. It was not long after they settled in Plas Newydd that the 'Ladies', in spite of their life-style, philanthropy and in particular, the peculiarity of their dress, became accepted within Llangollen's society and they were visited by many. Soon their life of 'friendship, celibacy and the knitting of blue stockings' was regularly interrupted by producing lavish meals for such famous visitors as Sir Walter Scott, Wordsworth, Shelley and the Duke of Wellington (the latter's mother was a member of the Trevor family of Bryncynallt, Chirk). It became customary for guests to bring a present of carved oak or a curio as a thank-you for the welcome they received at Plas Newydd. Soon the house was full of intricate carved pieces and many of them continue to adorn the house today. The year 1809 brought a great sadness to their lives when Mary Carryll, their loyal and trusted housekeeper, died. She was buried in Llangollen near the church and the 'Ladies' erected a fine three-sided memorial over her grave. As the years passed by, the 'Ladies' became more set in their ways with their odd masculine appearance and dress becoming more pronounced. They always wore well-cut, superbly tailored riding habits in either black or blue and 'beaver' hats, their hair being cut short and powdered. With advancing years, although still able to be relatively active, they were unable to accomplish as much as they wished. This was particularly true of Eleanor, who was the eldest, but right up to 1828 they were able to continue their daily walk up the valley, spending the remainder of the day in the garden and their library. In the early summer of 1829, Lady Eleanor Butler died leaving her friend and lifetime companion devastated. The town of Llangollen also felt a great loss at her passing and on the day of her funeral, all the shops closed as a mark of respect. Sarah Ponsonby continued to live in Plas Newydd in spite of being overwhelmed by loneliness. She busied herself in trying to sort out their papers for she had a premonition that she would not survive many years without her 'Beloved'. In December 1832, Sarah died and joined her two friends in Llangollen's churchyard. Plas Newydd is now open to the public and one can enter into the world of the 'Ladies of Llangollen' who lived a life-style far ahead of their time but were, nevertheless, loved and respected by the people of Llangollen. Today they are very much a part of Llangollen's history and continue to draw visitors to their beautiful home. As one leaves Plas Newydd, Castell Dinas Brân (Dinas Brân Castle) perched high on its isolated hill on the opposite side of the valley makes a dramatic backcloth to the house.

Returning to the town, the steep hill soon joins the A5. In his book *Llangollen and its Vicinity* (1827), W. T. Simpson describes a similar scene: 'Besides the London Mail to Holyhead, which passes through Llangollen every afternoon at five o'clock, and leaves the letter bags, which it takes up again about eight o'clock every morning, there are regular stage

The ruins of Castell Dinas Bran above the Vale of Llangollen. [WAW]

coaches passing to and from London and Holyhead every day.' The mode of transport may have changed, but Llangollen continues to welcome its visitors and this is made obvious every year during the first week of July when the International Musical Eisteddfod takes place. This is an unique festival of song, dance and music with competitors from many countries across the world filling the town. The first International Eisteddfod was held in 1947 and was seen at that time to be a positive attempt, after the horrors of the Second World War, to bring together people of many nations to share their music and culture in a spirit of goodwill and friendship. Since those early days, the Eisteddfod has become one of the main events of the year in the Welsh cultural calendar. In recent years a new permanent pavilion, has been built above the town, alongside the canal, and on its stage a kaleidoscope of music and dance is performed to enthusiastic and appreciative audiences. Outside the pavilion, people of many nations, resplendent in their national costumes, mingle with visitors young and old, from home and abroad, who come to enjoy not only the music and dance but also to experience the feeling of sharing something special. During Eisteddfod week, the town residents, together with people from the surrounding area, throw open their doors to provide accommodation for the competitors. The competitive aspect to the Eisteddfod seems to be a secondary factor to an appreciation of the different traditions and culture that each competing group brings to the stage. The Eisteddfod has now developed not only a programme of varied music, dance and singing competitions, but also offers evening concerts with renowned international stars from the world of music. There is no doubt that the hard work of the Eisteddfod organisers, together with their many supporters, is continuing to achieve the words of the Eisteddfod motto 'Blessed is a world that sings. Gentle are its songs.'

One could say that Llangollen has been blessed with its location. Not only is it situated on a main route from London to Ireland, but it has one of Wales' most beautiful rivers flowing through it, a canal providing leisurely boating and now a renovated railway station and railway line giving visitors the opportunity to explore the Dee valley a little further. The station, situated over the bridge on the north side of the town was, before the demise of many railway lines in the early 1960s, an important link with the western seaside resort of Barmouth, the line considered to be one of the most beautiful in Britain. In addition, the line was also used to carry goods. In the mid 1980s, a group of rail enthusiasts decided the time was right to open up the line once more and much work has been done to re-lay the tracks. The line is now run by the Llangollen Railway Trust who have successfully re-laid the tracks from Llangollen up to Carrog, providing a daily service not only for tourists but also for locals. Special events are organised from time to time during the year with 'Santa Specials' and 'Thomas the Tank Engine' weeks being particularly enjoyed by children. Adult rail enthusiasts can arrange to have a 'Driver Experience' and 'Dining Events' provide an unusual social evening whilst travelling through the magnificent scenery of the Dee valley.

Situated high above the railway station is Llangollen Wharf with a sweeping view of the river and the town below, surrounded by wooded hills. The building now houses the Canal Museum and Exhibition Centre which traces the history of the canal and displays examples of 'canal

The Horseshoe Falls on the Dee above Llangollen, photographed c.1910. [WAW]

ware', the colourful objects used by the bargees on their boats and painted in the traditional way. The canal was constructed by Thomas Telford as part of a plan to link the River Dee to the River Severn through a canal system, but the scheme was not completed. Nevertheless, the new stretch of canal to Llangollen proved to be profitable for a time but with the coming of the railway system, goods were transported at a greater speed. This brought about the decline of canal transport and affected not only Llangollen and the surrounding area, but also numerous towns in England that were linked to the canal system. After many years of disuse, the Llangollen canal was rescued by a group of enthusiasts who set about clearing and cleaning it up, eventually re-opening it as a tourist attraction. The wharf is once again a busy terminus for the many boats which now use the canal – it possibly sees more traffic now than it ever did. Although the canal flows upstream for a further two miles, touring boats are only able to progress about fifty yards beyond the wharf to the last place where they can turn around. For those who wish to continue further, horse-drawn barges tow visitors during the summer months upstream towards the Horseshoe Falls.

As an alternative to this leisurely cruise, a walk along the tree-lined tow path provides a variety of interesting things to see. Very soon the canal passes the International Eisteddfod Pavilion on the outskirts of the town. Glimpses of the river, and at certain times the train, can be seen through the trees as the town gives way to more open countryside with steep hills rising up ahead. At Pentrefelin, the walker can pause and visit the Motor Museum which is housed in buildings which used to be part of the old wharf, serving as a terminus for the tramway which carried slates from the quarries high up on the slopes of the Horseshoe Pass during the mid-nineteenth century. Now the canal runs through rock cuttings and the river Dee appears below, rushing over black, shiny rocks. Ahead is a low building, the Chain Bridge Hotel, with its chain-linked suspension bridge crossing the cascading waters.

The Chain Bridge Hotel is a popular stopping-off point for walkers and those who have travelled by barge. The hotel provides an excellent viewing point to see enthusiastic canoeists taking up the challenge of the 'white water' of the Dee which flows below, especially during the autumn and winter months when the river is in full flow. In the past, the International Canoe Championships were held every mid-October on this stretch of the river but, unfortunately, they have now been moved to a new venue in Cardiff Bay. Nevertheless, the local canoe club, and other clubs from far and wide, still enjoy the challenges of the rushing, fast-flowing waters of the Dee surging over its rocky river bed.

Spanning the river at this point is the chain bridge, the third bridge to have been built here. Known as the Berwyn Bridge, the first span was built c.1814 by one Exuperius Pickering, an unusual name for an unusual man according to local records. He was not only known as one of the 'iron-masters' of the time, but was also one of the 'coal-kings' which resulted in his being extremely wealthy. Despite his money, he was always on the lookout for ways to extend his businesses and fully aware of the potential of the iron and coal industries in the area. Not wanting rival businesses to take over, he decided to safeguard his enterprises by constructing a foot-bridge over the river so that the coal that came up the canal could be transported at this point over the bridge onto the new A5 road being built by Telford. It could then be transported higher up the valley to Corwen and even beyond, as far afield as Bala.

Despite the constant rush of water against its support pillars, Pickering's bridge survived for over fifty years. By 1870, however, it was beginning to show signs of disrepair and it was decided to construct a new bridge. This was done by Henry Roberston, one of the owners of the Brymbo Ironworks. Robertson, a skilled engineer and builder of bridges and railways, constructed the second bridge based on a similar design to the first bridge, that is, two mid-river supports carried by chains below the decking. In February 1928, the area suffered storms and flooding, large trees were swept from upstream until they came to the Berwyn Bridge where they jammed against the pillars of the bridge forming a dam. More trees and rocks were carried down causing further pressure against the bridge, eventually these, together with the turbulence and force of the water, destroyed the bridge's supports and it was swept downstream. A year passed before the third bridge was built, the chain bridge we see today. Built in the form of a supension bridge by Sir Henry Robertson, son of the second bridge builder, it is thought to be a miniature replica of the Menai suspension bridge built by Thomas Telford to link the Isle of Anglesey to the mainland. Unfortunately, much use and the affects of time and weather on the timber walkway have forced the bridge to be closed. In recent years, the new proprietor of the hotel has shown a keen interest in repairing the Chain Bridge so that it can link the hotel with the now renovated railway station of Berwyn on the other side of the river. The hotel owner has confirmed that the bridge has now been 'gifted' to Llangollen Town Council and the nearby Llantysilio Parish Council who are working together to commence the repair and renovation work on the bridge. Plans are now in place, and with the help of European funding, this remarkable bridge will become another attraction in this beautiful valley in the near future.

On the opposite bank from the hotel and bridge is Berwyn Station, now re-opened as a busy halt on the recently re-established Llangollen Railway. Immediately upstream from the chain bridge, the canal tow path arrives at a valve house, which is where the canal starts its journey. Here, the water from the river Dee is measured and controlled as it flows into

The ruinsof the Cistercian abbey at Valle Crucis. [WAW]

the canal. Beyond the valve house, a path leads through a field to the Horseshoe Falls, which is in fact an arc-shaped weir built by Telford to supply water to the canal. Because the canal is fed by the river, it is popular with anglers as it has a variety of coarse fish in it such as roach, perch, pike and carp. The canal, together with the river Dee and its salmon, makes the valley a virtual paradise for the enthusiastic angler. Despite its shallow drop of approximately half a metre, the Horseshoe Falls with its elegant curve framed by overhanging branches, and a backdrop of the bracken-covered slopes of Llantysilio Mountain and the wooded lower slopes of the Berwyns make this a very popular place, especially during the summer months when visitors and locals can enjoy a picnic on the grassy river banks. A short walk from this spot is the old church of Llantysilio, sheltering within a circle of trees. Dating from the fifteenth century, with major restoration work carried out in 1869, the church has many interesting features including a fine medieval roof, a rare medieval oak eagle lectern, and an intricately sculpted font. Some of the windows retain their original stained glass and the exterior of the north wall has fragments of an earlier twelfth-century building incorporated into it. It is said that the poet, William Wordsworth, read a sermon here and that, at a later date, Robert Browning worshipped here. Browning's visit is recorded on a plaque inside the church. Near the entrance to the churchyard is the grave of Exuperius Pickering, the builder of the first Berwyn footbridge, who died in 1835. There is no doubt that Llantisylio, and its neighbour Berwyn, have a beauty and tranquility of their own and, although less renowned than Llangollen, are in the words of H. L. V. Fletcher: 'equally worthy of notice.'

To return to Llangollen, one can choose a variety of options – catch the train at Berwyn Station and enjoy the experience of a steam-train journey, take the horse-drawn barge along the canal or walk the tow-path. There is, however, one other historical gem to visit before returning to Llangollen. Leaving Llantysilio Church turn right along the B5103, on approaching a junction, turn left onto a path leading into woodland above the road. Fine views of the Eglwyseg and Trevor Rocks together with Dinas Brân Castle can be seen through breaks in the trees. The path eventually comes to the A542 Llangollen–Ruthin Road which climbs up steeply over the Horseshoe Pass. Approximately one-hundred yards up it is necessary to cross the road with care and follow the waymarked path down to Valley Crucis Abbey.

It was founded in 1201 by Madog ap Gruffydd Maelor, prince of

Powys, for the order of Cistercian monks and said at one time to be the largest monastery in north Wales. Although the ruins now share their peaceful setting with a nearby caravan park/camping site, the magnificence of the architecture helps eliminate this twentieth-century intrusion. Nestling in the shelter of hills, it is not hard to imagine why such a place was chosen, its setting was one of peace and tranquility for the monks, the hillsides provided pasture for their sheep and the nearby river Dee gave ample supplies of fish. Iolo Goch, poet to Owain Glyndŵr and one of the greatest poets of his day, is buried here. Unfortunately, during the thirteenth century, the abbey was ravaged by fire but it was rebuilt and survived until Henry VIII destroyed it with his policy of dissolving religious houses.

In a field above the caravan park, just off the A542, are the remains of a ninth-century cross. Set on a grassy mound believed to be an ancient burial chamber, it is known as Eliseg's Pillar. The rounded shaft becomes square at the top but the upper portion of the cross is missing as is the lower portion. The original height would have been about twice the present eight feet. During the Civil War, it was knocked down and broken, but re-erected in its present form in 1779. Its original Latin inscription was transcribed in 1696 and revealed that the stone was erected by Cyngen, king of Powys, in honour of his great-great grandfather, Eliseg. The valley in all probability takes its name from Eliseg's Pillar, becoming known as the Valley of the Cross and later giving the name Valle Crucis to the monastery.

Before leaving Llangollen, reference must be made to Dinas Brân Castle, the imposing ruin which looks down on the town from its lofty perch of over 320 metres. For keen walkers, an exhilarating walk up its steep grassy slopes is rewarded with splendid panoramic views. On a clear day, it is possible to see Snowdon in one direction and the Wrekin in Shropshire in the other. The castle ruins have recently undergone major repair and renovation, nevertheless an air of mystery and romance continues to enhance this spectacular ruin. It was built on the site of an ancient iron-age hillfort by Gruffydd ap Madoc, one of the reigning princes of Powys, sometime before 1270. Despite its favourable position and strength, the castle's military career was short lived. During 1277, Edward I's invading army progressed through the Dee valley with the intention of taking Dinas Brân but found that the castle had been deliberately burnt by its Welsh garrison to prevent its use by Edward's forces. As a result, an English garrison was placed there, its commander commenting that Dinas Brân was potentially the mightiest fortress in Britain. The castle eventually passed back into Welsh ownership but was never rebuilt.

There are many stories linked to Dinas Brân; even before the castle was built, the hillfort was linked to a legend alleging it to be the haunt of ghostly giants guarding golden treasures. Its name, probably meaning 'the crow's fortress', has been linked with Brân the Blessed, a Celtic hero-god and even with the Holy Grail. One story, however, tells of love, passion and heart-break. It is said that Myfanwy Fychan, the daughter of one of the wardens of the castle, was strikingly beautiful and many handsome young men journeyed to the castle to praise her beauty and seek her favour. Myfanwy, however, rejected them one by one for not one of them had the gift of composing poetry and music which reflected her beauty. One day a young bard, by the name of Hywel ap Einion, entered the castle together with other suitors. When he began to sing his poetry to his harp accompaniment, his skill and talent outshone his rivals. His words praising Myfanwy's unrivalled beauty together with his haunting melodies attracted Myfanwy's attention and she ignored all other attempts to woo her. Hywel was greatly encouraged, every day he climbed the steep slopes from his home in the valley below to praise the beauty of Myfanwy, his true love, in the hope that one day she would return his love. Myfanwy continued to be enchanted by Hywel's words and music until one day a wealthier, more handsome suitor came to the castle, his words and music excelling those of the young bard Hywel who was subsequently ignored and forgotten by Myfanwy. Heartbroken, Hywel climbed no more to the castle on the hilltop but wandered the woods of the Dee valley singing laments to the love he had lost.

The road from Llangollen to the next of the 'Seven Wonders' winds eastwards towards Wrexham. Initially, it is bound by the river on one side and the canal on the other, sheltered by a canopy of trees. Soon it opens up as the valley broadens with the Trevor Rocks rising high above the road on the left with the lower slopes of the Berwyns meeting the A5 road on the opposite side of the valley. An old coaching inn, The Sun Trevor, provides a welcome break for walkers, canal cruisers and other passing travellers, its large windows providing spectacular views of the valley.

As the road enters Trevor, it is worthwhile making a slight detour to the Trevor Basin. Now a busy centre for canal boat cruising, it is easy to imagine the hustle and bustle of activity when the canal served local quarries, collieries, ironworks and brickworks during the nineteenth century. For those with a head for heights an exhilarating walk can be taken across Pontcysyllte, Telford's spectacular aqueduct. The tow path runs along one side of the canal guarded by a strong handrail. The height of the aqueduct can be truly appreciated by looking down over the handrail to see a ribbon-like river Dee threading its way between thickly wooded banks. Ahead, the canal stretches eastwards to link up eventually with the Shropshire Union Canal.

On leaving Trevor, the landscape becomes suddenly industrialised with the villages of Acrefair, Cefn Mawr and Rhosymedre, once reliant upon iron-smelting and coal. As this area developed during the nineteenth century, many collieries were established, each one supported by a vibrant village community. The village of Ruabon was an important manufacturing centre for the production of fine ceramics, bricks and tiles. The red Ruabon brick, with its fierce red colour, has adorned countless buildings in Wales and far beyond. On the outskirts of the village, set in impressive parkland laid out by Capability Brown, stands Wynnstay Hall, formerly the principal residence of the Williams-Wynn family which had immense estates and were regarded as the richest and most powerful in north Wales during the eighteenth and nineteenth centuries. Such was their influence, wealth and impeccable Welsh pedigree (the estate having passed down by descent from Madog ap Gruffydd Maelor, the founder of Valle Crucis Abbey) that some members of the family merited the unofficial title of 'The Prince in

Wales'. The building we see here today is one of many to have been built on this site. As the family's influence waned during the twentieth century, the hall became Lindisfarne College in 1950 and, when the school closed some years ago, the estate was taken over by a developer and now the hall, together with its out-buildings, has been converted into luxury homes. Despite this, Ruabon, particularly the centre, continues to have something of the character of an estate village. On the main road against the churchyard wall is the Round House, an eighteenth century circular lock-up used for local prisoners. St Mary's Church dates mostly from 1870–2, but with a fourteenth-century tower, has some interesting interior features and memorials.

Before progressing on to Wrexham, a short detour to the village of Rhosllannerchrugog, known locally as 'Rhos', is well worth a visit. Situated on the lower slopes of Ruabon Mountain, Rhos is a sprawling village which evolved as a mining community during the nineteenth century and once claimed to have the largest population of any Welsh village. First impressions of Rhos are its narrow streets with houses snuggling up against each other with no apparent thought given to planning. It seems that owning one's house was a prominent ambition for the miners and they built their houses on small plots of land whenever they became available. The majority of the men worked in the nearby Hafod Colliery whilst the women were at home reigning supreme, keeping the home clean and tidy and preparing meals for the family. In many ways, this reflects the character of the inhabitants of Rhos, fiercely independent, proud individuals, strongly family orientated. Another feature of Rhos is the great concentration of Nonconformist chapels in the village, many of which are impressive examples of chapel architecture, with some denominations having more than one chapel. There is no doubt that the presence of these places of worship had a great influence on the cultural traditions of the community. The chapel provided a place where the whole family could share, not only spiritual support, but the opportunity to socialise. Most of the chapels held meetings during the week for children and adults and it was here that many were introduced to the choral singing for which Rhos is renowned.

In addition to this, Nonconformism influenced other aspects of Welsh life such as politics and education and the inhabitants of Rhos have shown an enthusiasm for these over the years.

In the centre of the village stands the Miners' Institute, a large, imposing building of Ruabon brick, built with money raised by the community in the 1920s. Here the local choirs gave their choral concerts, the debating society met to discuss not just local politics but any issue which affected society generally, drama groups rehearsed and performed here and a cinema brought the latest movies, albeit months after their first showing in towns and cities elsewhere. The 'Stiwt', as it is affectionately called, was the hub of the village's cultural life. During the latter part of the twentieth century, however, with the closing down of local collieries and outside influences creeping in, the village may have lost some of its original character. The beloved 'Stiwt' has been refurbished and attracts concerts, plays, children's shows, lectures and poetry readings, plus a variety of community-based activities. Despite many of the old traditions disappearing, Rhos continues to hold onto its culture and its special atmosphere of time and place, making it an unique village. There is a choice of roads leading out of Rhos to Wrexham, each one gently descending down the hillside to the main Llangollen – Wrexham road. On a clear day, the the town of Wrexham can be seen in the distance as one descends, with the next of our 'Seven Wonders', the tower of St Giles' Church, rising high above the rooftops.

Wonder 3
Wrexham Town – WREXHAM STEEPLE –
Bersham – Clywedog Valley – Erddig

ONCE A SMALL MARKET TOWN, Wrexham is now the major centre for shopping and commerce in north Wales. Records show that a market existed here in the Middle Ages and, as early as Tudor times, substantial town houses were being maintained here by the local gentry. As to the origins of Wrexham, history does not throw any light on this and many researchers have looked in vain for a geographical or strategic reason for the town's foundation. If there was indeed a settlement here during the time of the Roman occupation, there is very little evidence of this apart from the remains of a Roman farm found during excavation work prior to the Plas Coch retail park being built in the 1990s on the outskirts of the town. It seems the Romans were more interested in nearby Holt where a large Roman camp was established. Following the Roman withdrawal, however, Wrexham became disputed territory with the native British holding on to the highlands and the Anglo-Saxons making advances from the plains of Cheshire and Shropshire. Such were the territorial disputes along this border land that two of the kings of Mercia, which lay to the east of Wales, saw fit to build huge linear earthworks to protect their settlements along this borderland. King Ethelbald of Mercia (AD 716–57) attempted to create a visible frontier in his construction of Wat's Dyke, the remains of which can be seen in Erddig Park and, to the west of the town, in Garden Village, a pre-1914 housing development, where the remains of Wat's Dyke skirt its western boundary. One of the streets was named Wat's Dyke Way as it is very close to this ancient earthworks and in 1977, a new primary school was opened and named Wat's Dyke School. From here, remains of Wat's Dyke can be seen in an area called

Wilderness Wood on the banks of the river Alyn on the edge of the recently established Alyn Waters Country Park which was once the site of a sand and gravel quarry. As a result of this, any early settlement in Wrexham would have become part of the kingdom of Mercia. Despite this attempt to create a boundary between Wales and Mercia, borderland disputes continued under the leadership of the princes of Powys who ruled the land to the east and south of Wrexham. By the year 780, Mercia was ruled by Offa and he made a final effort to define the whole western frontier of Mercia by erecting Offa's Dyke which stretched for 149 miles from Prestatyn in north Wales to the Severn Estuary, east of Chepstow, in south Wales. Although the Welsh in part agreed to this, Wrexham and the lands to the east still remained in Mercia and several attempts were made to regain the territory over a period of many years. As the authority of Mercia weakened, the Welsh, under the rule of Gruffydd ap Llywelyn, advanced against the Mercian forces and in a fierce battle at Rhyd-y-Groes near Welshpool in 1039, defeated the enemy. His support for regaining lost border lands encouraged persistent raids and eventually under his rule, the Welsh broke through Offa's Dyke in many places pushing the frontiers eastwards. This resulted in Wrexham and disputed land north and south becoming part of Wales again with the river Dee becoming the new border. Wrexham has remained within Wales since those turbulent times but continues to retain its identity as a border town.

If little is known about Wrexham's early origins it seems that even less is known about the origin of the town's name. Many theories have been put forward by numerous local historians but none have agreed as to how the name was derived. What is agreed, however, is that the second syllable 'ham' is the Saxon word for settlement. The name appears in old documents in many forms – Wristleham, Wrettesham, Wrechessam, Wryxham, Wrixwm, Rixwm, Gwrexam, and Gwraigsam – with the earliest identifiable reference being in 1161. A possible simple explanation is that it is a combination of Latin and Anglo-Saxon signifying the 'King's hamlet'. Despite the confusion surrounding the town's early history, it is known that from 1086 to 1277 Wrexham and the surrounding area formed part of the native Welsh kingdom of Powys

Fadog. Because of its close proximity to the border, the town experienced constant threats and occupation from the powerful earls of Chester. As the Norman occupation was consolidated along the border, its influence became more acceptable to the native princes and lordships were created. The lords of Maelor held lands stretching from Dinas Brân in Llangollen to beyond Marford where the river Dee became the eastern boundary. The lordship was divided into two commotes, one at Wrexham and the other at Marford. Wrexham was further divided into two manors, Wrexham Abbot – belonging to the abbot of Valle Crucis Abbey, and Wrexham Regis – belonging to the king. During the thirteenth century, the lordship of Maelor, together with other Welsh lordships, was subjected to stronger pressure as the Anglo-Normans extended their hold over the whole of north and west Wales. New shires were established under Edward I's Statute of Rhuddlan in 1284 but the borderland lordships of north-east Wales were not included but were, instead, created into new independent marcher lordships with Wrexham becoming part of the lordship of Bromfield and Yale. In spite of the increasing influence of the English, Wrexham was able to retain much of its Welsh character and began to establish itself as a market town and an administrative centre.

The rule of the Marcher lordships remained strong until the Tudor dynasty succeeded to the English throne. Many of the local rulers had become unruly and made little effort to maintain law and order within their lordships. King Henry VII became dissatisfied with this lack of authority and made positive attempts to remedy it but his untimely death in 1509 delayed the implementation of any significant changes. With the ascension of Henry VIII, the days of the marcher lords were well and truly numbered. The passing of the Act of Union in 1536, saw these lordships abolished and grouped together to form new shires or counties. The lordship of Bromfield and Yale, of which Wrexham was a part, was absorbed into the new county of Denbighshire.

Wrexham's prosperity expanded as a result of the Act of Union. Merchants and traders were allowed to travel further afield and the town became an important market centre, holding two markets a week plus frequent cattle sales. The town's March Fair was noted throughout north Wales and across the borders into nearby Cheshire and Shropshire and, until the mid nineteenth century, was the largest fair of its kind selling a wide range of goods. Traders from the industrial towns of England also moved into the town for the March Fair, setting up trade halls or markets. Hardware dealers came from Birmingham and traders selling Yorkshire cloth were regular visitors. Many of the town's covered markets were built on the sites of these old trade halls. For example, the still existing covered Butchers' and General Markets and the demolished Vegetable Market were built in the area of the town known as Birmingham Square, later renamed New Yorkshire Square, in the mid nineteenth century. Only two of the original covered markets have survived to the present day with the new People's Market built in the 1990s continuing Wrexham's market tradition. The open air market is still held every Monday. Wrexham's early prosperity was not to last and the town entered a turbulent period with an increasing influx of ruling families from across the border.

The Dissolution of the Monasteries in 1535 was no doubt a catalyst for much bitterness and enmity in Wrexham as the old faith was outlawed and its parish church became caught up in the struggle between the Roman Catholic and the newly-established Protestant Church. Resulting from this, the town saw the persecution and subsequent execution in 1584 of Richard Gwyn, the first Welsh martyr to the papal cause. Born a Protestant, Richard Gwyn converted to Catholicism whilst a teacher at Overton, a village not far from Wrexham. His attempts to spread his new faith brought him many enemies forcing him to move from place to place. He was eventually caught in Wrexham in 1579 but managed to escape. His freedom, however, was brief and he was caught for the second time in July 1580 and imprisoned for four years. Eventually, he was brought to trial, charged with high treason and sentenced to death. According to local records, he was at one point taken to the parish church in chains and forced to listen to a sermon. This did not deter him and he protested by rattling his chains causing constant interruption throughout the sermon. On the day of his execution, he was dragged from his prison cell along the High Street and Charles Street to the area known today as the 'Beast Market', where he was tormented prior to being hanged, drawn and quartered.

Early in the seventeenth century, Wrexham was caught up in the struggle between the established church and the rise of Puritanism which was supported by many influential families who felt that the Church of England was becoming too closely aligned once again to the Church of Rome. The church was also caught up in the political troubles which swept through north Wales as the Civil War took its hold.

Although Wrexham was strongly aligned to the Royalists in the early years of the war, Parliamentary soldiers entered the town in 1643 and took over the church, using it as a stable and also a prison. It is said that they melted down the pipes of the church organ to make ammunition. The vicar at that time, who unfortunately preached against Cromwell and his forces, was dragged from the pulpit and deprived of his living. He was replaced by Morgan Llwyd, who as a boy had been educated at Wrexham Grammar School and fallen under the influence of the Puritans. He returned to north Wales as an itinerant preacher in 1644 and as the Puritan movement gained a considerable following, was appointed non-episcopal vicar of Wrexham Parish church in 1656. Although an eloquent preacher, it is thought that Morgan Llwyd rarely preached or conducted a service in the Parish Church preferring to preach in the open air in various places in and around the town. Not only was he an outstanding theologian but he was also a prolific writer publishing eleven books, three in English and eight in Welsh, of which the most important *Llyfr y Tri Aderyn* (The Book of the Three Birds). Published in 1653, it is still regarded today as a classic of Welsh literature. Morgan Llwyd died in 1659, at the relatively early age of forty, and was buried in the Dissenters Graveyard in Rhosddu, on the outskirts of the town. There is no doubt that his influence continued after his death and helped the town's Nonconformists to remain strong despite persecution. As a result, Nonconformity became and still remains a dominant feature of the religious life of the town and surrounding areas. In 1912, the town paid homage to Morgan Llwyd by unveiling a monument to him on the supposed site of his grave and the town's first Welsh-language secondary school carries his name.

Although religious and political conflicts continued to influence life in Wrexham for the greater part of the eighteenth century, the town was becoming more and more a centre for a number of industries starting up in the local area. One of the first to recognise the area's potential was John Wilkinson who in 1762 took over his father's iron foundry at nearby Bersham. This was developed further in 1793 by the establishing of a smelting works at Brymbo. Years later, this became the site of the Brymbo Iron Works (later Steelworks). The lead industry was also being developed and rich seams of coal were mined on the western side of Wrexham. Within the town itself, industries such as tanning and brewing were established. Unfortunately, over the years many of these old industries have disappeared resulting in the need to find a diversity of new industries many of which are sited out of town on industrial estates making a valuable contribution to the wealth and future development of the area.

Today, the parish church of St Giles still stands on its prominent town-centre site and boasts another of the 'Seven Wonders of Wales'. Rising to a majestic 136 feet, the church tower has been the dominant feature of the Wrexham skyline for more than five centuries and is worthy of its inclusion in the old rhyme. Situated just off the High Street, and protected by handsome gates made by the Davies brothers, skilled craftsmen from nearby Bersham, the church was described by Sir Gilbert Scott, the architect of Liverpool Anglican Cathedral, as 'one of the finest specimens of its kind' and he implored 'that no one should be allowed to alter it in any way.' Records show that a church has been present on this site since the thirteenth century. The first church, possibly with a wooden tower, was wrecked by a storm in November 1330. The second church was probably built by the monks of Valle Crucis Abbey, as it stood on land then owned by them. It is known that the church contributed part of its income to the Abbey as far back as 1220. Unfortunately, a large part of this church was destroyed by fire in 1463. There are, however, traces of the Decorative style in which it was built still to be seen in the

The magnificent parish chuch of St Giles, Wrexham. [WAW]

present church which was built in the late fifteenth century in the Perpendicular style, with the church tower having many outstanding features. The tower is crowned with four turrets of differing heights and has five levels each of which is enriched with carved figures, both human and animal, each one within its own niche. There were originally thirty of these niches but now only twenty-eight are visible. Despite its height, the carvings at the top of the tower are as skilfully carved as those on the lower levels. Above the north porch is the carved figure of St Giles accompanied by a deer which, according to legend, nurtured the saint when he was in the wilderness. The figure of the Virgin Mary is in a nearby niche, its presence another reminder of the close connection between the church and Valle Crucis Abbey in the early days.

On the lower section of the west side of the tower can be seen a stone with the following carved into it: 'THIS STONE REPLACES ONE PRESENTED TO YALE UNIVERSITY, USA, 1918.' The original stone from the tower was gifted and placed in a replica tower built on the campus of Yale University which was founded as a direct result of the generosity of Elihu Yale, who lived at Plas Grono on the outskirts of Wrexham. The Yale family was one of the respected families of the old county of Denbighshire, the name Yale being originally 'Iâl' after an old Welsh *cantref*. Elihu Yale's parents left the ancestral home, Plas yn Iâl, in Bryn Eglwys, and moved to America where Elihu was born in 1649. On returning to England in 1652 the family settled in London where Elihu was educated and later, as a young man, gained valuable experience in his father's business before gaining employment with the East India Company. He proved to be a shrewd and enthusiastic businessman and in about 1676 was sent to Madras in India to work for the company. Before long, his skills brought him great wealth and influence and he became governor of Madras. Whilst in India, he made frequent visits to London, very often interrupting his voyage in Africa, a country he became very fond of, taking an interest in the wildlife and culture of this continent. In 1699, he left India having been made a governor of the East India Company and divided his time between London and his home in Plas Grono. Elihu Yale proved to be a generous benefactor to Wrexham

Parish Church, donating many gifts including the beautiful screen and gates in front of the church altar and a painting in the ante-nave at one time believed to have been painted by Rubens. When he heard that money was required to establish a university in America, the land of his birth, he donated a large sum of money which resulted in the new university being named Yale University. This historical link between Wrexham and Yale University continues to bring many American visitors to the town and the church. Elihu Yale died in London in 1721 and was buried in Wrexham Parish Churchyard, to the west of the church tower His tomb is inscribed with the following epitaph:

Born in America, in Europe bred,
In Africa travell'd and in Asia wed,
Where long he liv'd and thriv'd, in London dead,
Much good, some ill he did, so hope all's even.
And that his soul, thro' mercy's gone to heaven,
You that survive and read this tale take care,
For this certain exit to prepare,
Where blest in peace and action of the just,
Smell sweet, and blossom in the silent dust.

The tomb of Elihu Yale in St Giles churchyard, Wrexham. The stone presented by Yale University can be seen in the church wall behind. [WAW]

When a new college of further education was established in Wrexham town centre some years ago it took the name of Yale College, a fitting tribute to a man who, in spite of his travels, valued his close links to the town and the area. Unfortunately, Yale University in America objected to the college's name and threatened legal action. As a result, the new Yale College changed its name to Yae College Wrexham.

Only one major addition has been made to the Parish Church since 1520 – the south-west porch built in 1822. The interior of the church was improved in 1867 by replacing the old box pews with the pews we see there today and replacing the wooden triple pulpit with a stone pulpit. A fine example of the work of the sculptor, Louis François Roubiliac, can be seen in the memorial to Mary Myddleton of Croesnewydd Hall who died in 1747. The church has many fine stained-glass windows – the east window tracing the lineage of Jesse is brilliantly coloured. The west window, in the lower part of the tower, was presented to the church by the Royal Welch Fusiliers when their regimental chapel was established in the church. It shows a remarkable richness of colour. Another window with an interesting history is the one dedicated to the memory of Bishop Heber who wrote the old missionary hymn 'From Greenland's Icy Mountains' whilst staying at the old vicarage and it was sung for the first time in the Parish Church on Whit Sunday 1819.

The narrow streets around the Parish Church have many buildings retaining their original architectural features and the broad High Street boasts a number of eighteenth- and nineteenth-century three-storey buildings on either side. The Wynnstay Arms Hotel at the bottom of the High Street was originally a small inn called 'The George' dating back to the late seventeenth or early eighteenth century. It was later enlarged and took the name of 'The Eagles' which it kept until the mid-eighteenth century before taking the name 'The Wynnstay Arms' when the property came into the ownership of the Williams Wynn family of Wynnstay Hall, Ruabon. Threatened with demolition in the 1960s, local opposition saved the day with the frontage of the building being preserved whilst a complete reconstruction took place at the rear. Prior to the sport being banned in 1835, a bull-baiting post was sited in the street in front of the

Wynnstay where, on a weekly basis, a bull would be tethered to the post where it would be baited by dogs brought in by gentlemen from the surrounding countryside. The hotel's original name, the Eagles, has recently been resurrected and given to the new retail complex built at the rear of the hotel and opened in autumn 2008, taking the name Eagles Meadow. Up until 1940, the old Town Hall was situated in High Street near to its junction with Hope Street and Town Hill. An earlier building, dating back to 1562, had stood here originally with a number of shops at ground level around an open space with a large room above, known as the Grand Chamber, which was used when the Great and Quarter sessions were held. The Chamber was also probably used to hold courts of the old manor of Wrexham Regis, together with those of the manors of the lordship of Bromfield and Yale. This hall was replaced in 1713 by a new building on the same site, the upper floor being supported by arches resting on pillars creating a covered open space with no shops. Unfortunately, as time progressed, a permanent use for the old Town Hall was not found and it fell into disrepair, becoming a victim of the town's new developments in and around this old site.

There is no doubt that Wrexham's growth and prosperity has been influenced by the many industries which flourished in and around the town over the centuries. In 1762, the village of Bersham, became one of the cradles of the Industrial Revolution when John Wilkinson, together with his brother William, took over the ailing furnace from their father, Isaac, who had been involved with the iron works here since 1754. Due to plentiful supplies of coal and ironstone, plus water to supply power, Bersham was probably operating in the seventeenth century, if not earlier. It took the genius and energy of John 'Iron Mad' Wilkinson, however, to develop new methods of heating the furnaces with coke thus accelerating the process. As a result, Bersham was soon in the forefront of the industrial changes of the era and covered an area of almost half a mile in the Clywedog valley and employed over 400 men, women and children. Due to the number of international conflicts during the latter half of the eighteenth century, the demand for iron ordinance grew rapidly which John Wilkinson was able to meet successfully. His invention of a machine to bore cannon and cylinders out of iron put Bersham in the forefront of this industry. Not only did Wilkinson use his boring mill to produce armaments but he also modified the machine in 1775 to bore cylinders for James Watt's new improved steam engine. Such was the quality of Wilkinson's steam engine cylinders that Watt wrote in 1776, 'Mr Wilkinson has improved the art of boring cylinders so, that I promise upon a 72ins. cylinder being not further from absolute truth than the thickness of a thin sixpence in the worst part.' The works continued to expand into the 1790s but, when John purchased the nearby Brymbo Hall Estate in 1793, where he intended setting up another iron works, a quarrel erupted between him and his brother. Things went from bad to worse and by 1795, the Bersham works was put up for sale. John Wilkinson bought his brother's share but, because he was now concentrating on developing Brymbo, his interest was already in decline. The quarrel between the Wilkinson brothers was never resolved and when they both died in 1808, a nephew attempted to revive production but his success was limited and the works were finally sold in 1812. The site, together with various buildings, were put to a variety of uses after the decline of the iron works. Gradually, many of the buildings fell into disrepair with only a few surviving into the twentieth century.

Clwyd County Council purchased the site in 1988 and commenced on an ambitious archaeological dig, as a result of which the remains of a substantial iron works were revealed including a blast furnace and coking ovens which had disappeared behind later farm buildings. Because of the importance of the site in relation to the Industrial Revolution a decision was made to create a Heritage Centre based on the ironworks and today visitors can see John Wilkinson's story unfold in the Centre's museum. A short walk away the 'sights and sounds' of the ironworks have been recreated at Bersham Mill. It also provides a valuable education service offering a wide range of teacher resources and, from time to time, interactive programmes where children can re-enact working in the ironworks, dressed in costumes of the period, under the watchful eyes of their strict taskmasters played by local actors.

The Bersham Heritage Centre is also the base for the Clywedog Trail

John Wilkinson, ironmaster. [WAW]

which was opened in 1991 linking the many industrial sites of the Clywedog valley, all linked by the river Clywedog which provided the water power for the various industries. The river rises high above the valley on Minera Mountain before making its way downstream to eventually join the Dee. Until the last quarter of the nineteenth century, its waters powered nineteen or more mills along its course. One of these mills, namely Nant Mill, has been renovated in recent years and is now a popular visitor centre and a starting point for a number of local nature trails. The mill organises a variety of educational programmes relating to the history of the mill and to the flora and fauna found in the surrounding area. It also houses a man-size mole tunnel which fascinates both young and old.

Higher up the valley, at the start of the Clywedog Trail, is the village of Minera with an association to lead mining that goes back to Roman times. Midway between Minera and Nant Mill is the scattered village of Coedpoeth which translated literally means 'hot wood' which, according to some, relates to the time when the area was densely wooded and early charcoal-burning activities were carried out here to smelt the lead mined at Minera. Offa's Dyke runs through the lower part of the village where parts of it are still visible. Coedpoeth was the centre for some of the very earliest coal mines in the area with records showing a charter was granted as early as 1410 for coal to be dug in the 'wastes' of Coedpoeth as it was then described. Although now a populous dormitory village to nearby Wrexham, Coedpoeth together with Minera have played an important part in the industrial development of the region.

One cannot leave Wrexham without visiting Erddig Hall, situated to the south-west of the town. Now owned by the National Trust it provides a rare insight into the life of a grand country house. Built between 1684 and 1687 for Joshua Edisbury who, having been appointed High Sheriff of Denbighshire in 1683, felt it necessary to build a house which reflected his rising status within the county. Unfortunately, his financial circumstances did not match his social status and he had to borrow large sums of money from local gentry such as Elihu Yale. Edisbury's continued extravagance forced him into greater debt and he was eventually forced by his creditors to sell Erddig to John Mellor, one of his principal creditors, and it was he who completed the construction of the house. Mellor was a man of taste and, having no money problems, was able to furnish Erddig with fine pieces of furniture. When he died childless in 1733, the house and estate passed to his nephew, Simon Yorke. From that time through to 1973, there has always been either a Simon or a Philip Yorke as 'master of the house' at Erddig.

Over time, the house was extended and improved, particularly during the time of the first Philip Yorke, during the eighteenth century. When the last Simon Yorke, a bachelor, died in 1967 the estate passed to his brother Philip. Unfortunately, the house and many out-buildings had fallen into disrepair and there was a severe problem with subsidence due to the mine workings beneath the house. The once immaculate gardens were also overgrown and the surrounding parkland lacked management. The new 'squire', Philip Yorke III, feared for the continued survival of the Erddig estate, knowing full well that if its degeneration continued it would become a crumbling ruin and its unique contents scattered far and wide. After much negotiation, Philip Yorke gifted Erddig to the National Trust in 1973. The house, gardens and parkland were opened to the public four years later and quickly became one of the most fascinating houses in Britain. Its atmosphere is that of a lived-in country house with all its family treasures and bric-a-brac carefully restored. There is also an aware-ness that the family of the house had an unusually close relationship with their servants, confirmed by the numerous portraits of staff which are displayed around the walls of the servants' hall, each accompanied by a descriptive verse written by the first Philip Yorke and Simon Yorke II.

Eighteenth-century print of Erddig Hall. [WAW]

Outside, the various outbuildings evoke images of how the house relied on the skills of their workers making the estate an efficient, self-sufficent unit. The walled garden has been restored to its eighteenth-century formal design, whilst the extensive parkland provides a variety of interesting features and walks. Situated on the northern boundary of the parkland is the site of a motte and bailey castle which was constructed against Wat's Dyke on an elevated site above the river Clywedog. This was referred to as 'the castle of Wristleham' in the Pipe Rolls of 1161 and is possibly one of the earliest references to the name of Wrexham. In his book *A Tour in Wales*, Thomas Pennant, the eighteenth century traveller records his visit to Erddig: 'I pursued the track of Wat's dike, ... and soon reached Erddig, the elegant feat of Philip Yorke, esq. a place where nature has been lavish of beauties, and improved by the excellent taste of its owner.' Pennant's words are no doubt echoed today by the thousands of visitors who wander its gardens and parkland and enjoy the unique atmosphere of the house.

Wonder 4

Marchwiel – Erbistock – OVERTON YEW TREES – Bangor-on-Dee – Holt

NOT FAR FROM ERDDIG (which we visited in the last chapter) is the fourth of the 'Seven Wonders' to be visited, namely the ancient yew trees at Overton. The short journey takes us through lush farmland towards the village of Marchwiel, a village of early origins said to be linked to the extensive monastic settlement which existed at nearby Bangor-on-Dee from around 170–615AD. Edward Lhuyd, the great Welsh scholar, confirms in his *Parochialia*, published in 1699, that Marchwiel supported an early church belonging to the monastery at Bangor-on-Dee, known as Daniel's Chapel (Daniel being Deiniol in English). It is known that Deiniol was the son of Dunawd, the abbot at Bangor. Marchwiel's early church probably survived into the Middle Ages but there is no written record of when the church became dedicated to St Marcella. What is certain, however, is that a church has survived on the site of the present building from at least the thirteenth century until the late eighteenth century when it was rebuilt by the parishioners. The tower is said to be reminiscent of the tradition of Sir Christopher Wren's London churches and village hearsay has the great man staying in Wynnstay Hall in Ruabon and suggest he may have been asked to design the tower. Unfortunately, records show that Wren had died before the church and tower were rebuilt. The church interior was completely refurbished in the 1920s and in the late 1960s after it had been scheduled as a building of historic and architectural interest. A Restoration Fund was set up in order to safe-guard it from the ravages of time and the death-watch beetle. Fortunately, the restoration work was completed successfully and the many memorials housed within the church remind the visitor of its links with the Yorke family at nearby Erddig.

The delightful Georgian church at Marchwiel. [WAW]

Records indicate that Marchwiel was part of the lordships of Bromfield and Yale in the Middle Ages. Prior to that it was regarded, even during the Anglo-Saxon period, as very much a border village with Offa's Dyke marking the boundary between Wales and the kingdom of Mercia only a short distance to the west. Over the years, the area saw a steady flow of Welsh settlers moving across the dyke to the more fertile farmland near the river Dee and, with the increasing power of the Welsh princes, Welsh law and tribal customs prevailed. When the Normans created the lordships of Bromfield and Yale, the Welsh influence in legal and administrative matters continued with the names of the ancestors of the Broughtons of Marchwiel Hall and the Sontleys of Sontley becoming prominent. These two families, together with the Edisburys and the Yorkes were to play an important role in the later history of the village and the county.

During the Second World War, Marchwiel made a vital contribution to the industrial fortunes of Wrexham when a large Royal Ordnance Factory was built on requisitioned farmland on the outskirts of the village. This has now developed into the vast complex of the Wrexham Industrial Estate and boasts a diversity of new industries replacing the now long-gone traditional industries of coal and iron.

On leaving Marchwiel, the A528 road meanders through rich, fertile, farmland towards Overton-on-Dee. The River Dee flows through the landscape at a gentle pace and is crossed by the impressive, stone Overton bridge. Situated on the bank of the river, above the bridge, is the Cross Foxes dating from 1681. Now altered and modernised, it is a popular inn and restaurant with particularly good views of the bridge from its terraced gardens. Behind the 'Cross Foxes' a narrow road winds its way to Erbistock with its sandstone church situated above the river. The church, dedicated to St Hilary, is said to be the third church built on this site. Church records show that an earlier building was present in 1692, the present church dating from 1861. Was there, however, a church or Bede-house set up on this site at a much earlier time? As Erbistock is relatively near to Bangor-on-Dee, where we know there was an early monastic settlement, there is a strong possibility of an earlier church having stood here. It would be reasonable to assume that a monk from the Bangor settlement, seeking solitude, could have established a small church here, on the banks of the Dee, probably of wattle and daub construction. Records indicate that this early building was dedicated to St Erbin, a Celtic saint, making it the only church in Wales dedicated to him. Although no mention of a church is made in the Domesday records, the completion of the Norman conquest saw the Welsh church system destroyed, the Normans demanding obedience to Canterbury which resulted in the re-dedication of many existing churches. Erbistock church could have been re-dedicated to St Hilary at this time. The present church was rebuilt as a memorial church. Relatively small in size, its exterior shows some features of Gothic church architecture. The interior boasts intricate carvings on the pillars, particularly on the arcade capitals and has a rather impressive brass chandelier, a gift from the Kenrick family of nearby Eyton Hall. Other features in the church, such as the reredos and the west window, were gifts given in memory of the Boates family, an old Erbistock family. Beyond the church, nestling on the river bank, is the old 'Boat Inn', a late seventeenth century inn with its garden sloping down to the water's edge. At this point, the river Dee makes a sweeping loop between steep, wooded banks before flowing under Overton bridge. Until 1939 it was possible to cross the Dee by ferry from the Boat Inn where the ferry was hauled across the water by a winch, the remains of which can still be seen on the river bank. This section of the river offers good fishing and it is known that coracles were used for salmon fishing on this stretch of water, possibly into the twentieth century.

Erbistock has a number of large houses still remaining, such as Erbistock Hall, Manley Hall and Rose Hill, all reminders of an era when the land was made up of estates owned by Anglo-Welsh gentry or wealthy business families moving in from Cheshire and Shropshire. These estates contributed much to the farming and social life of the community, their names remain as much a part of the area as the land itself. Returning along the road from Erbistock, the tall four-storey building of Erbistock Mill comes into view, its origins date from 1602. No longer a working mill, it would have been, in its hey-day, the focal point for the surrounding farming community. Glimpses of Overton bridge can be seen through breaks in the trees, its graceful arches reflected in the deep waters of the Dee. An earlier bridge was built about one and a half miles below the present bridge. The present site, however, has been in use since the end of the seventeenth century when a wooden bridge was originally constructed. The upkeep of the wooden bridge proved to be a constant expense resulting in a plan to replace it with a stone bridge. The original stone bridge, with a single arch, was designed in 1810 but unfortunately collapsed in 1813 whilst still under construction. A new design, with two arches, was completed in 1815 and has survived to this day. After crossing the bridge the landscape on the left opens out into rolling parkland dotted with tall, stately trees. This land was part of the Bryn-y-Pys estate which owned most of the land and buildings in and around Overton in the past. The estate was owned over many generations by the Price family, with the original hall dating back to the sixteenth century. Old records of 1808 mention, however, that: 'a new

Erbistock ferry, c.1900, now the Boat Inn. [WAW]

mansion had been built at Bryn-y-Pys, Overton, in the county of Flint, and completed in 1807. The house-warming party for the opening of the new house had been quite an elaborate affair, there had been a masquerade and a dinner afterwards attended by the local gentry.' Unfortunately, on the death of Francis Richard Price in 1853, the estate was sold. At that time, it was one of the largest estates in the area, being in the region of 2,000 acres. It was sold to one Edward Ethelston who changed his name to Peel in 1857 after he purchased the estate. The Peel family (relatives of Sir Robert Peel, prime minister and founder of Britain's first police force) lived in Bryn-y-Pys mansion until 1955 when the deteriorating condition of the building necessitated its demolition. A gatehouse, just off the roadside, leading into the parkland has survived, but one can only imagine the grandeur of the Georgian mansion that once overlooked this landscape. The name Bryn-y-Pys and that of the Peel family still remain very much a part of the village of Overton and its church.

It is believed that a motte and bailey castle stood on the high ground above the park, its exact position is not known but it was probably built in 1155 by Madoc ap Maredydd, prince of Powys Madog. Maps indicate an area known as 'Castle Hill and Wood', an elevated position overlooking the river, the Dee Valley and the Cheshire plain, making it a perfect site for a castle. Records also confirm the castle's existence in 1349 and reference is made to it by Leyland, the Tudor travel writer and antiquarian, who visited Overton in the sixteenth century and referred to the castle as a ruin.

Many visitors to this area of north-east Wales feel that it has a more 'English' rather than 'Welsh' atmosphere. This is possibly due to the fact that Overton is situated only a few miles from the border with Shropshire. Prior to 1974, the village was in the detached part of the old county of Flintshire known as Maelor Saesneg (English Maelor). This strange territorial arrangement came about during the reign of Edward I who wished to create new Welsh counties in an attempt to establish some order over the Welsh princes. Problems arose, however, with the territories of the Marcher lords for they had shown loyalty and support to Edward and he felt he could not take their lands. Consequently, he left much of the border country as independent lordships. In 1283, Maelor Saesneg was restored to the Crown, becoming part of the county of Flintshire. Further territorial complications arose when Henry VIII finally suppressed the marcher lordships, dividing their lands between the Welsh counties. He gave the great lordships of Bromfield and Yale, to the county of Denbighshire, whilst Maelor Saesneg became a detached part of Flintshire. In spite of this detachment, the area (including Overton and other villages) has developed a particular character of its own, made up of well-farmed and well-managed land belonging to big estates.

It is said that the name 'Overton' comes from the Anglo-Saxon, meaning 'an upper settlement'. This is feasible for the village is situated on a headland of red sandstone high above the river Dee. The settlement of Overton passed to Robert Fitzhugh, a reward to one of William the Conquerer's most loyal followers, and it is mentioned in the Domesday Book. For a period during the twelfth century Overton was in the hands of Gruffydd, prince of Powys, who on his death bed passed it to his son Madoc ap Gruffydd. During Edward I's reign, the village passed back into the hands of the English, and in 1286 was granted a market by the king who also made it a free borough. Markets were held in the village well into the nineteenth century with a weekly Saturday market and four annual fairs held on specific dates in the year. Overton was on the old drovers' route from Wales to the Midlands and the south of England which brought additional trade to the village. 'Holland pit', a pond situated outside the village is the only remaining local evidence that drovers stopped to rest and water their cattle here. Droving was an important and prosperous trade for Wales between 1300 and the second half of the nineteenth century, but the development of railways and improved road transport brought about its demise. In spite of many centuries of English influence, it is surprising how many Welsh names of houses and farms have survived in and around Overton. The Bryn-y-Pys estate is one example, but others such as Argoed, Pen-y-lan and Pen Dyffryn also remain as reminders of Overton's Welsh heritage.

There is no doubt that Overton's border village situation gives it dual characteristics, making it in many ways rather special, and to find another of the 'Seven Wonders of Wales' within its boundary – the yew trees mentioned in the old rhyme – is no surprise. Once you are in the village High Street, there is no missing them, their rich evergreen foliage contrasting with the red sandstone of the church tower. On approaching it becomes obvious that these apparently ancient trees create a complete circle around the church. Known to be definitely 400 years old and possibly 640 years old, they are now protected by a Preservation Order.

Yew trees have had a very close connection with churchyards for many centuries and also had a particular significance for Druids, who regarded the yew as a magical plant. For many, the tree is also regarded as a symbol of mortality. In Wales, some yew trees were consecrated and in certain areas, it was customary to place yew branches with the body in the grave and then to decorate the grave with yew. As the wood of the yew was particularly suitable for making longbows many were grown within the safe confines of churchyards. This ensured a constant supply of the wood to make the bows of Welsh archers who became important elements in Welsh armies and who, from time to time, played a major role in the armies of English kings. Although there are numerous ancient yews to be found in other parts of Wales, Overton yews have become famous as a result of their being listed amidst the 'Seven Wonders'.

The church, encircled in its evergreen enclosure, is an impressive building dedicated to St Mary. It is more than likely that the site of the present church goes back to the seventh century, when a wattle and daub Christian oratory stood here. Mainly Perpendicular in style, the present building still retains some ancient features in spite of major renovation in 1870. One of the oldest features is a Norman circle cross, built into the western pillar of the nave, on the right as one enters the church. A number of sepulchral slabs dating from the early thirteenth and early fourteenth centuries are visible reminders of the first stone church built here, and of the later enlarged fourteenth-century church. During the 1870 renovation, not only was the church further enlarged, but much of its interior was re-modelled. The old box pews were replaced and a new steep hammerbeam roof replaced the old nave roof. Further renovations

One of the ancient yew trees in Overton churchyard. [WAW]

were carried out in the early 1920s when the organ and choir stalls were moved, together with the pulpit lectern which dates from 1637. In 1935, new oak choir stalls were installed, each one elaborately carved by a parishioner, Evelyn Wybergh, who also carved the statue of the Virgin and Child situated in the side chapel. Another example of her work is the war memorial. Situated on the pillar near the pulpit is a very unusual processional cross on which is carved the crucifixion and other scenes. Originally brought from Abyssinia, where it seems a number of these crosses, dating possibly from the sixth century or even earlier, were thrown onto a scrap heap. Rescued by soldiers of Queen Victoria's army campaining in Abyssinia, one of the crosses has found a home in Overton parish church. The church also boasts three fine stained-glass windows by William Kempe, the Victorian artist. The church has been, and still is, a focal point of community life and is very proud of its place in the village's history. In recent times Overton's population has grown, with many new homes being built in and around the village, and fortunately it has succeeded in retaining its village atmosphere and environment.

Although many visitors come to Overton to see the yew trees, there are many other interesting and historical buildings and features to be seen. A walk around the village, following the village trail, provides the visitor with an opportunity to view other aspects of its past. On leaving the church, a path leads through the churchyard, where many old gravestones record the names and trades of past generations. To the rear of the church stands a weather-beaten shaft of a fourteenth century churchyard cross. Leaving the churchyard, and looking back, one has a fine view of the church guarded by its ancient yews. To the rear of the church is School Lane leading to the school which was established in 1848 as a National School. A first attempt at providing free education in the village was made as early as 1800, but records show that education was available long before this date in the form of private schools (or dame schools). One famous village schoolmaster was the young Richard Gwynn who converted to Catholicism during his time in Overton. As history tells us, his new faith later cost him his life, becoming Wales' first Catholic martyr. He is remembered in Overton's Catholic Church which is named after him and also in the beautiful stained-glass window inside the church. The old National School served the village well into the twentieth century, when the new St Mary's School was built in 1987. Further along School Lane are a number of interesting buildings, one has its windows bricked up reminding us of the period of 'window taxes' when householders were taxed on the number of windows in the buildings they owned. Near the end of the lane is Quinta Cottage, a black and white, timber-framed building of the type built during the seventeenth century. This is a type of domestic architecture very popular over the borders in nearby Cheshire and Shropshire and it is therefore, not surprising to see it in Overton. At the end of School Lane, Turning Street presents a mixture of old and new dwelling houses, complementing each other, adding to the character of the village. Just before reaching High Street the last building on the left with its carved gable boards, the striking features of its windows and row of tall, diagonally-set chimneys, provides yet another example of old domestic architecture. At this point, it is possible to appreciate the breadth of the High Street straight ahead, and imagine the bustle of fair days held here in the past, when it became the focal point and meeting place for villagers and traders.

On the opposite corner stands a very impressive house known as 'Pendas'. Dating from the eighteenth century, its three storeys of red brick has dignified proportions which blends surprisingly well with the row of adjacent cottages on the Wrexham Road, dating from the same time. The cottages arched windows and pointed doorways project a rather Gothic appearance, but the warm colour and texture of the small hand-made bricks, gives them a homely look. All of the cottages are now protected as listed buildings, so their unusual yet neat appearance, full of character, will remain for future generations. On the other side of the Wrexham Road, but set back from the road, is another row of similar cottages, with what was once the old smithy incorporated at one end of the row. Set further back is a building of very fine proportions known as Park View, which, dating from the nineteenth century, has many interesting architectural features. The adjacent building known as Peel

House has a memorial plaque to Edmund Peel of Bryn-y-Pys. Opposite is a very formal entrance leading to a fine avenue of trees with the village cricket ground running alongside. Cricket has always been a popular sport in the village since the middle of the nineteenth century, but other sports have also been well represented.

The river Dee has always been popular for its fishing and it is known that coracle fishermen earned their living on the river until about 1920 with a street in the village being named Coracle Terrace at that time. Both the Price and the Peel families of Bryn-y-Pys enjoyed a variety of sporting pastimes with hunting, shooting, fishing and horse racing being very popular. Their stud farm at nearby Argoed, and estate farm, housed some of the best blood-stock in the area and they were the instigators in 1859, for setting up horse racing at nearby Bangor-on-Dee.

The Peel family won great acclaim in the racing world when a horse they had bred won the Grand National in 1918 and 1919. The horse, named 'Poethlyn', was sold and at one time used to pull a milk float. Fortunately someone with an expert eye noticed it and felt it had a better future on a race course. The Peel family were informed and advised to buy the horse back. This they did with the result that 'Poethlyn', carrying the yellow and blue colours of the Peel family, ridden by the jockey Ernest Piggott, grandfather of the famous Lester Piggott, rode to success in the most prestigious race in the horse-racing calendar. 'Poethlyn' is buried near the spot where the Bryn-y-Pys mansion once stood, a sandstone headstone marking his grave. The horse is also commemorated in the village where a row of houses along School Lane is named Poethlyn Terrace.

Leaving the parkland and returning to the Wrexham Road, a short walk to the right brings one to the Anne Maria Peel Memorial Chapel, built in the nineteenth century by Edmund Peel in memory of his wife. Once known for the quality of its stained-glass windows, it is now, unfortunately, roofless and in a state of severe disrepair. In spite of this, its stone spire survives together with some fine stone carving around the door. An adjoining cemetery was opened to the village in 1872. Returning to the village via Willow Street, one is surprised once again at the variety of domestic architecture which has survived over time. The street's environment is further enhanced by the well-kept gardens and well set out tree planting.

Ahead the church tower can be seen above the dark foliage of the yew trees and nestling alongside the church is a small black and white cottage. The High Street is made up of buildings whose scale and design are varied and contrasting, many dating from the eighteenth century. The White Horse Inn is a prominent example of Cheshire half-timbered style, dating from the early eighteenth century, with some earlier work visible here and there. Serving as a coaching inn in its early days, it continues to extend a warm welcome to locals and visitors. At the southern end of the High Street, a number of attractive buildings on Pen-y-Llan Street, together with some magnificent horse-chestnut trees, creates a feeling of enclosure, giving the street the semblance of a village square. Situated on Pen-y-Llan Street is a building with an unusual name, Cocoa and Reading Rooms, dating from 1890. Such buildings came about as a result of promotion by temperance societies and by the Quakers who controlled a great part of the cocoa market. The rooms at Overton were built by Edmund Peel of Bryn-y-Pys who had become increasingly worried that the instances of drunkenness amongst the villagers was getting out of control. He thought that this fine new building would encourage the villagers to become interested in a variety of activities as an alternative to drinking. What level of success was achieved to diminish this problem is not known, but the building serves as a reminder of Edmund Peel's generosity and his concern for the welfare of the villagers. Around the corner from the Cocoa and Reading Rooms is Salop Road along which stood another old coaching inn, named the Bryn-y-Pys Arms. It is said to have been the venue for many celebrations in the past. The Price family of Bryn-y-Pys Hall used it often, one member of the family holding his wedding party there. Today, however, the coaching inn is no more, having been transformed into a small housing development with new dwellings built around what would have probably been the old coach yard. This development is aptly named Bryn-y-Pys Court. On leaving Overton along its broad High Street, one has a feeling of having had a glimpse into the past but also a glimpse into the life of a vibrant, modern village community, proud to be the home of one of the Seven Wonders of Wales.

There are several routes out of Overton leading to the next wonder, one of the most interesting being via the villages of Bangor-is-y-Coed (given the English name Bangor-on-Dee by the railway company in the nineteenth century) and Holt, along the B5069. Both these villages are similar to Overton in so much that they are near the border with England with the river Dee flowing through them. Bangor-is-y-Coed was also once a part of Maelor Saesneg, the detached part of the old county of Flintshire. According to historical records, the first monastery in Britain was established here in the second century and there are many legends relating to this, and there is no doubt it was a place of importance in the history of the early Celtic church.

One such story relates that 2,000 monks lived in the monastery and a specific number of them took turns to pray throughout the day and night. There is some doubt that such a large number were housed here for no substantial archaeological evidence has been found to support the existence of such a large monastic community. What is known to be true, however, is that in the sixth century the Celtic church refused to accept the authority of Rome which angered Augustine whose mission was to set up the Church of Rome in Britain. Dunawd, the then abbot of Bangor, became the spokesman for the Celtic church against the continued pressure from Rome. As a result of this resistance, it is said that Dunawd and the monastery at Bangor became the prime targets of Augustine's wrath, and he sought to take revenge. Conveniently for Augustine, Aethelfrith, the Anglo-Saxon king of Northumbria, marched onto Chester in 615 in an attempt to overcome the native British. On learning of this, Abbot Dunawd summoned his monks to pray that the Anglo-Saxon army be defeated. Aethelfrith interpreted the monks' prayer as an act of aggression against him personally and ordered the monks to be slain and the monastery at Bangor destroyed. A small number of monks managed to escape and they made their way to Bardsey Island, off the western tip of Gwynedd, where they established a new Christian com-

*Bangor-is-y-Coed Church, c.1900. The house on the right has
now been demolished. [WAW]*

munity, a safe distance from the mainland. The name of Abbot Dunawd
is remembered in the village's parish church which is dedicated to this
brave, early Christian and it also reminds us of Bangor's links with the
Celtic church.

Nowadays, Bangor-is-y-Coed is more familiar with race-goers who
attend race-meetings held here during the National Hunt season.
Established in 1859, it was for a period, the only racecourse in Wales. The
first race was held in order to settle a wager between the Honourable
Lloyd Kenyon and Richard Myddleton Biddulph. As a large crowd turned
out to witness the race, it was decided to make it an annual event with
local farmers and members of Wynnstay Hunt competing. Over the
years, the amenities have been improved and extended, but the racing
takes place over virtually the same course as the very first event. Situated
on pleasant farmland, in a huge loop of the river Dee, it continues to
attract many race-goers who enjoy its rural atmosphere.

Not far from the race course is the very fine, restored, medieval

Bangor-is-y-Coed Bridge. [GAJ]

Althrey Hall. Prior to its purchase in 1986, it had been virtually abandoned and in a very severe state of disrepair. The new owner began the painstaking job of replacing or restoring the oak timbers within the hall, and during the work uncovered many clues to its history. One interesting feature is the existence of a small chapel on the first floor which has a painted ceiling representing the Celestial City, and a disguised entrance leading into a priest hole.

The village of Bangor-is-y-Coed is located at an important crossing point of the river which is spanned by a five-arched sandstone bridge dated 1658. Now too narrow for modern traffic, a one-way system has been devised so that the bridge is not overstressed. Crossing the bridge on foot reveals the 'refuges' on the parapets where pedestrians could retreat to avoid being crushed by cattle or teams of packhorses crossing the Dee in earlier times. The church of St Dunawd stands on the river bank, close to the bridge, its sandstone tower reflected in the deep waters of the river below. The church was badly damaged in 1643 during the

English Civil War and was restored in 1723, enlarged in 1832, and with further work carried out in 1877. Opposite the church is the 'Royal Oak', a black and white inn of half-timber structure. The streets of the village are narrow with several old, interesting buildings here and there. On the outskirts of the village are a number of housing developments which have increased the population of the village over the years.

Leaving along the B5130, the road passes through an area which is particularly rural and obviously very reliant on the land, with large farms set amidst green fields and small communities huddled along the roadside. Over centuries, this land had been in the forefront of the power struggle between the Welsh princes and the invading English forces as a result of which many place names are a mixture of both Welsh and English, with echoes of the feudal system of the past still evident throughout the area.

The village of Holt, however, has a history and character all of its own. A medieval township with its old bridge, a ruined Norman castle and an ancient church, its history goes back to Roman times. Situated on the banks of the river Dee, Holt's position was a strategic and significant point on the border between Wales and England and was the scene of many conflicts over the centuries, particularly on or near the bridge. The Dee at this point acts as the border and was originally crossed by ferry before a wooden bridge was constructed in 1319. The present sandstone bridge, of eight arches, dates from the fourteenth century. At one time, the bridge had a building on it, some say it was a gatehouse with drawbridge, others, that it was a small chapel dedicated to Our Lady. The second suggestion is supported by the fact that one of the arches of the bridge is known as the Lady's Arch. It is possible that the bridge was built on the site of a more ancient river crossing dating back to Roman times.

Records reveal that a small Roman settlement was established in Holt, linked to the larger and more important Roman legionary fortress of Deva, modern Chester. The reason for the Roman interest in Holt, which is ten miles up river from Chester, was the substantial amounts of clay, sand and gravel, the materials necessary to make tiles which the Romans used in their buildings. The river provided a convenient means of

Holt Bridge. This was once fortified with a gated tower. [GA]

transport and very soon a large tile manufactory was established on the banks of the Dee at Holt. Remains of the workshops and tile making equipment have been unearthed over the years.

After the departure of the Romans, Holt maintained its position as a strategic point on the river and witnessed periods of great turmoil over many centuries. Its Norman castle, situated on the banks of the Dee, dating from the thirteenth century, became a focal point of the power struggle between the Norman lords and the Welsh princes. Later, during the English Civil War, it fell alternately into the hands of the Royalists and the Parliamentarians. Holt, in keeping with the majority of north Wales at that time, was supportive of the king, with Cheshire, just across the river, supporting the Parliamentarians. After being besieged for twelve months, Holt Castle was eventually taken in 1647, and from then on, time and the ravages of weather have resulted in its decline. It is now a ruin with only fragments of walls, on a five-sided plan, poised on a rock, around and against which the castle was built.

The church of St Chad was built at about the same time as the castle.

Situated on higher ground above the river, it has survived the ravages of time more successfully than the castle, having been restored more than once. Approaching the church through the main gateway, its symmetrical proportions, its impressive battlemented tower, flanked by yew trees, makes a pleasing picture against the skyline. Parts of the nave, the chancel and the tower belong to the thirteenth century with further extensions being made some two hundred years later. The interior of the church reflects much of Holt's history – its octagonal font (dating from 1493) is elaborately carved with the heraldic arms of the lords of Holt Castle, and is accepted as one of the finest examples of ecclesiastical furniture to be found in north Wales. On the west wall is evidence of Holt's involvement in the turmoil of the English Civil War in the form of marks made by soldiers' bullets. Until the church restoration of 1872–3, rushes used to be strewn on the church floor on Rush-bearing Sunday, the first Sunday in August, where they remained until the week before the first Sunday in August of the following year.

To this day, parts of Holt still retain features of the old medieval township, granted a charter in 1411 which was confirmed by Elizabeth I in 1562, when it became a royal borough. Standing in the centre of the village, on what was in the past a large open space, is the market cross. Now only the shaft remains, mounted on a pedestal, with six steps leading up to its base. From here the burgesses carried out their business transactions during the annual fairs and weekly markets. Annual hirings were also held here. Markets continued here until 1872. It would be from the steps of the Cross that all public proclamations and announcements were made. The Cross remains a focal point in the village today, with the majority of the village businesses set around it.

There are many interesting old houses in Holt, one being 'The Academy', built as a schoolroom by the Revd Ebenezer Powell in the nineteenth century. The school flourished and produced many eminent scholars, but it is also well-known as the place where the writer H. G. Wells spent time as a teacher. Unfortunately, according to local history, Wells was not particularly happy during his time in Holt and his stay was short-lived.

Many old families still remain in Holt and the surrounding area, their names recorded in the township records as far back as the seventeenth century. One family, the Speeds, was related to John Speed, the historian and cartographer, born across the river in Farndon in 1542.

In spite of the turbulent history surrounding the castle and bridge, Holt has been and still is, a centre for a thriving agricultural community. Surrounding the village are vast fields growing crops of soft fruits and vegetables. These, together with farming, have sustained the village over centuries but, when the nearby Wrexham Industrial Estate was established, alternative employment became available. Locals and visitors alike can still enjoy Holt's strawberries by visiting Bellis Brothers' Country Market, where a variety of fresh local produce is always available. During the strawberry season the shelves are a mass of strawberry punnets. For the more energetic, it is possible to go out into the fields and pick your own fruit, not just strawberries but blackcurrants, raspberries and gooseberries. In his book *Holt and Its Records Through the Ages*, local historian John Powell, included a description of 'Strawberry Time' in 1900–01, taken from the local records. It is interesting to note that at that time the Holt strawberry fields were considered to be the most extensive in the west of Britain. The pickers were known as 'dodgers' because they dodged about the country picking fruit, vegetables and hops. Young children were employed to go out into the fields as early as 4 a.m., armed with wooden clappers to scare away the birds.

Leaving Holt on the A534, the road passes some farm shops selling fruit and vegetables, whilst in the distance to the south, the tall chimneys and buildings of the industrial estate can be seen against the skyline. Much of the traffic along this road is heavy and fast, for one of the main routes into the estate branches off to the left.

On the right, the land was once part of the old township of Borras and in about 1200, Plas-ym-Mwras (Borras Hall) was built by Griffri ap Cadwgan, lord of Borras and its neighbouring township Erlas (located along Borras Hall lane). Over time, parts of the original hall were demolished, other parts renovated, but it has been recognised in a recent survey by the Royal Commission of Historic Buildings as '... one of the most significant late medieval houses to have come to light in recent years. It belongs to a small group of ambitious gentry hall houses in north-east Wales that were distinguished by box framing (rather than cruck framed), large halls and projecting wings. Indeed, the West Wing at Borras Hall appears to be the largest surviving timber solar wing in Wales'.

Just before the A534 reaches the edge of the built-up area of Wrexham, is Wrexham Golf Course and, beyond it, Borras Airfield, constructed, on land requisitioned by the Air Ministry, as an RAF station during the Second World War. Now a new link road, completed a few years ago, carries the A543 along the outer edge of Borras Park, a large private housing development built on land which was once part of the Acton Park estate. This estate, with its once impressive hall and parkland, was the home of the Jeffreys family from 1629 when Jeffrey ap Hugh, a judge on the north Wales circuit, who built the original hall and made Acton his home. When he died in 1622, his son John Jeffrey of Acton, who fought in the Civil War as a Royalist supporter, inherited the estate. He became High Sheriff of Denbighshire in 1655 and increased his estate by purchasing land in and around Wrexham, plus land near Shrewsbury. He is better known, however, as being the father of the famous George Jeffreys, the Hanging Judge, who was born at Acton Hall on 15 May 1645. A talented and ambitious barrister, George used his allegiance to King James II to further his status and, at the age of 33, was knighted. He later became the Lord Chief Justice of England in 1683 and within two years was Lord Chancellor. His reputation as a cruel, ruthless man was highlighted when he sat in judgement at the trial of the rebels who had supported the Duke of Monmouth against King James II. Remembered as the 'Bloody Assizes', Lord Chief Justice Jeffreys handed out over 300 death sentences, and sentenced countless others to transportation and slavery. As a result of his cruelty, Jeffreys became a hate-figure and when William and Mary ascended the throne of England in 1688, he was placed in the Tower of London for his own safety. There he remained until his death in 1689. The Acton Estate remained in the hands of the Jeffreys

Judge George Jeffreys,
1st Baron Wem.

family until 1745, when it was sold. Eventually, and after several owners, part of the estate land was sold to Wrexham Borough Council who in 1920, built the first corporation housing development in north Wales.

At the end of the new link road it is necessary to follow the B5445 road through the round-about and on into Gresford where the next of the Seven Wonders can be seen. A short detour off the roundabout onto Bluebell Lane reveals the memorial to the miners killed in the Gresford Pit Disaster in 1934, when 261 colliers (plus three rescuers) died in one of the worst disasters in mining history. The memorial is the actual pit wheel from the Dennis shaft where the explosion struck. Returning to the B5445, the road soon enters the village of Gresford.

Wonder 5
All Saints Church – GRESFORD BELLS –
Gresford village – Marford – Rossett

FOR MANY YEARS, it was thought that the name 'Gresford' was an English translation of the Welsh word *'groesffordd'* meaning 'cross road' because of the existence, in earlier times, of a medieval wayside cross at the intersection of the old road from Wrexham to Gresford and the present B5445. This theory, however, is not substantiated by any written records. The eminent Wrexham historian, A. N. Palmer, however, suggests that the name is of old English origin, probably Anglo-Saxon, meaning 'grassy ford'. As modern Gresford is situated above the valley of the river Alyn, it is quite possible that an early settlement of Angles inhabited the lush meadows of the valley floor on the banks of the river where there would be a ford from which the settlement took its name.

The history of Gresford, however, does not start with the Anglo-Saxon settlement but goes back in time to the Celts, namely the Deceangli tribe who lived in this area of north-east Wales from 800 BC until Roman times. The Romans established a fortress at nearby Chester and made inroads into nearby Welsh territory setting up their tile factory in Holt, a farm at Plas Coch on the outer edges of Wrexham, and worked the shallow deposits of lead in Minera, obtaining the charcoal for smelting from nearby Coedpoeth. Noted for their road making, it is probable that they constructed routes from Chester to these places over the border with one of them passing through Gresford. As a result of this, some trading would have gone on between the Celtic inhabitants and the Romans. The Celts would also have assimilated some of the Roman customs and way of life. Evidence of this was found in Gresford when a Roman altar was excavated under the east end of the church in 1908. Nearly three feet high, it has a square base and four carved sides. Three of the sides have simple carved patterns with the fourth side depicting, in all probability, a Roman goddess. On the top of the stone is a depression where worshippers placed their offerings to her. Research has confirmed that this stone is similar to two other stones kept in the Grosvenor Museum in Chester and seems to be dedicated to the Roman goddess, Nemesis. Today, the stone stands inside the Parish Church in Gresford where acts of Christian worship have long since replaced this early form of worship. It is easy, however, to imagine that this carved altar stone, housed within a stone structure and set in a peaceful grove of trees, was an important aspect of the Romano-Celtic worship that possibly took place in Gresford in those early days.

Today's worshippers gather in the beautiful church of All Saints where the peal of church bells is recorded as one of the 'Seven Wonders of Wales'. Many consider this building to be one of the finest examples of church architecture in Wales. The tower, which houses the famous bells, rises gracefully above the yew trees which surround the churchyard. One of the trees, situated near the church gate, said to have been here since AD 500, surpasses all the others in its size and age, having a height of over eighteen metres and a circumference of over seven metres. It is more than likely that a simple stone church was built on this site at the beginning of the thirteenth century. At that time, it is probable that the inhabitants of Gresford were Welsh-speaking. During the Anglo-Saxon period, Offa, king of Mercia, had pushed the native Welsh of this area beyond the dyke which he had constructed, resulting in Gresford becoming part of his kingdom and speaking his language. Gradually with the strengthening influence of the Normans, who had their stronghold in nearby Chester, Gresford and the surrounding areas soon found their Anglo-Saxon way of life disappearing and they found themselves now influenced by three new Norman landlords appointed by Hugh Avranche, the Norman lord given control of Chester in 1070. The landlord responsible for Gresford, Osbern Fitztesso, held more land than the other two and was therefore more influential. In the Domesday account of 1086, it is recorded that the three Norman landlords were still holding the land granted to them with Gresford, referred to as Gretford, within the 'great parish' which included Holt, Rossett, Llay and Borras. The record concludes that 'Gretford' and its surrounding area was given a taxable valuation of sixty-five silver shillings indicating that it was a successful and well-run area. The village of Gresford had its church, its priest, a mill which provided the Norman landlord with a steady income, plus a number of people of middle-class social standing, in fact the village even at that time was showing a great potential to become socially and commercially viable. During the period 1070–1270, the Welsh began to return eastwards with the local Welsh lords agreeing to terms set by the earl of Chester who held the lands in and around Gresford. By 1250, things had improved and progressed to such a degree that the people of Gresford felt they could build and sustain their first stone church. Another incentive which encouraged their determination was that now they had their own Welsh bishop of St Asaph, replacing the bishop of Chester who had been responsible for appointing priests to the earlier church built on this site for the Norman landlord, Osbern FitzTesso. The 'new' church was built by local Welsh stonemasons having a pitched roof rising to about forty feet, using stone from the nearby quarry at Pont-y-Capel.

By the fourteenth century the church had become too small for its congregation and it was decided to add a second aisle along the south side. As there is no evidence of a tower being present at this time the church would probably have had one door on the west wall with three narrow windows on each side. The interior had a sanctuary raised slightly above the floor level with a crypt below it. Much of the finance needed to enlarge the church was provided by several affluent Welsh families who held lands in and around Gresford, most significantly, the family of Gronw ap Iorwerth ap David of Llay. This family, together with close relatives, had set themselves up in three great houses namely, Llay Hall, Pant Iocyn and Borras Hall, and their influence was felt throughout the parish. Inside the church are housed five memorials to various members of this family. In an arched recess in the north aisle, the impressive heraldic slab commemorates Gronw ap Iorwerth himself and

The beautiful interior of All Saints Church, Gresford. [WAW]

depicts a shield with a spear behind it and a mailed hand grasping a sword. Nearby is an un-named effigy, but its dress is that of someone of great importance, in all probability a judge, which is now believed to be a memorial to Sir David Hanmer who served King Richard II as sergeant-at-law and then as a justice of the King's Bench. His son, Sir John Hanmer, lived in Llay Hall and married the daughter of Gronw ap Iorwerth. On the south wall is the effigy of Madoc ap Llewelyn ap Griffri a relation of Gronw's through marriage. In front of this effigy are two further memorial slabs which are, unfortunately damaged. One of these stones, however, in spite of being buried for a period of time under the foundations of an old barn at Pant Iocyn, shows a carved shield with a lion rampant and a Latin inscription, which translated into English reads: 'Here lies Griffri ap ...' It is possible that he was a crusader; if not he was of high social rank. Once again, research identifies this man as Griffri ap Cadwgan who built Borras Hall and was grandfather to Madoc ap Llewelyn ap Griffri. No-one can be sure how this memorial stone came to be hidden at Pant Iocyn. One explanation is that it was removed there for safety to avoid it being destroyed by Cromwell's soldiers. What is known, however, is that Pant Iocyn, being the chief house in Gresford at that time, was best able to provide a hiding place for the stone. Today Pant Iocyn is known as Pant-yr-Ochain, a popular eating place. But why the change of name? According to some records the original name was Pant-yr-Ochain or Pant-yr-Ychain, the former meaning 'the hollow of sighs' and the latter meaning 'the hollow of the oxen'. According to Palmer in his book *A History of the Thirteen County Townships of the Old Parish of Wrexham*, Pant Iocyn is the true name, meaning 'Iocyn's hollow', Iocyn being a common personal name in those early times. The Pant Iocyn estate played a significant role in the history of Gresford and the surrounding townships, particularly during the time of the strong Welsh presence between the late eleventh and early fourteenth century. By the early sixteenth century, the house was owned by John Aylmer, an armour bearer and sergeant-at-arms to Henry VIII. During the next two centuries, the ownership of the house later passed into the hands of several influential local families and eventually became a farmhouse in

1730. Bought by Sir Foster Cunliffe, the then owner of nearby Acton Hall, in 1785, he decided to alter and rebuild part of the house around 1804–5.

The road from the Pant-yr-Ochain to Gresford passes a small lake whose waters lap the roadside. Known locally as the Flash, it is popular with anglers and used by the Gresford Sailing Club. It is referred to in old records and is known to have been used as a pleasure lake during the summer months by the past owners of Pant yr Ochain as far back as the seventeenth century. Edward Lhyud, the historian and botanist, made a survey of Gresford in 1699 and noted that this lake was '… one of the notable pools of the parish' containing a variety of fish such as tench, carp, dace and eels. The majority of these fish are still found in the Flash with only the dace having disappeared. At one point towards the end of the nineteenth century, however, the future of the Flash was in doubt as the water levels began to drop. Blame for this fell on the new collieries set up in the area as their pumps were sucking water out of the ground. The situation worsened when Gresford colliery started pumping in 1910 and the waters of the lake virtually disappeared. By 1919, however, for some reason not readily explained, the Flash began to fill up again and become a focal point for leisure activities in Gresford and the surrounding area. The name 'Flash', which is a Cheshire term for a stretch of water, was first used in the mid-eighteenth century when Gresford saw an increase in the use of the English language. Prior to this it had been referred to by the Welsh terms – *llyn* meaning lake or *pwll* meaning pool. A. N. Palmer records that the Flash was known as *Pwll Gwenllian* as far back as 1620 and according to local history, this name has strong political and historical links from an earlier period. Gwenllian was the daughter of Llywelyn, the last prince of Wales who, on the death of her father, was taken as a baby by King Edward I to Sempringham Priory in Lincolnshire where she remained a prisoner until her death in 1337. Perhaps the lake was named in her memory as it is known that Gronw ap Iorwerth of Pant Iocyn, and his kinsman Griffri ap Cadwgan of Borras Hall, were both staunch supporters of the Welsh princes. Their families continued to support them through to the time of Owain Glyndŵr.

Returning to the parish church, the extension of 1350 was built with stone hauled in from Cefn Mawr and New Broughton. The stone was carried in horse-drawn wagons belonging to hauliers who were required to provide their services and that of their assistants, who tended to be lowly Welsh labourers. In order to accelerate the building process the hauliers would have probably hired casual labour which resulted in the building work being completed in a relatively short time. The 'new' two-aisled church was about eight feet shorter than the present church but housed two very interesting features. One of these was the stone font situated near the south door, where it still stands today. Its design would suggest that it had come from the earlier church although there is no definite proof of this. Its eight sides are adorned with carved figures – King Edward the Confessor, St Sytha, St James, an angel with a scroll, the Madonna and Child, another angel and St Leonard. The presence of St Leonard is interesting as he is not familiar as a Welsh saint but recognised as a saint in France. Why is it that he has a such a prominent place on the font in Gresford church? The answer to this goes back two centuries. In 1161, a castle was built by Henry II at the Rofft, Marford, which was the neighbouring township to Gresford. The Welsh were beginning to threaten the security of Chester and the presence of this castle meant that he could keep in check any possible attack. The castle became an important centre for the Anglo-Norman administration of the area, with an appointed constable controlling the Alyn valley stretching from Marford to Gresford. As Marford did not have a church, it was decided that a small private chapel should be built in the valley to serve the castle which was named after a popular Norman saint, St Leonard. The chapel, situated in a secluded place in the valley was always referred to as 'St Leonard de Glyn' being a combination of Norman, French and Welsh words reflecting the presence of the Anglo-Normans and the Welsh inhabitants of the area. The chapel served the constable and members of his administration and was in continual use up until 1448.

Apart from the font there are numerous other features present in today's church which go back to the church of 1350. In those days, the church did not have seats and the congregation stood in the nave on a floor of beaten earth, covered with dry rushes. As there was no high pulpit the priest would stand on the chancel steps. The nave would be separated from the chancel by a rood screen usually supporting a great rood (cross). Behind this would be the choir stalls. It is these choir stalls, reflecting the superb skills of the woodcarvers, that provide another interesting feature in Gresford church. The tipping seats of the choir stalls are called *misericords* which is Latin for 'mercy seats'. When the seats are tipped up there is a narrow ledge underneath the seat which offered the choir and the priest the opportunity to half sit on them during the long church service which was the norm in those days. A prominent feature of the church service in those days would be the responses sung in Latin, alternating between the priest and the choir. In order that this could be done fluently, it was necessary for the choir members to see the priest directing the service and also the other members of the choir across the aisle. The misericords allowed the choir and the priest to relieve the pressure on their backs and legs by leaning against the misericord and yet still appear to be standing during these marathon acts of worship. The carvings on the Gresford misericords depict a variety of animals, both mythical and real, together with human forms. Some of them are quite grotesque but these are counter-balanced by the carvings of angels and bishops. It seems that the medieval wood carver used his skills to portray the hopes, fears and beliefs of the times in the images he carved on these seats.

There is no doubt that the church played an important part in the everyday lives of the inhabitants of Gresford and the surrounding area in those early days and, with its lively colourful ceremonies, brought the people together giving them relief from the miseries and hardship of every day life. The church year provided a series of processions and ceremonies relating to the various Christian festivals – Rogation leading on to Good Friday, Easter Day, Corpus Christi and later in the year All Hallows and Christmas. These holy days gave the villagers the opportunity to dress up in colourful clothes and wend their way from the church around the village accompanied by musicians beating drums, tambourines, blowing horns and bagpipes. The day's celebration would probably end up in the Griffin Inn, situated a short distance from the church and on land owned by the church. Although much altered, the Griffin is still a meeting place for the villagers of today, with its cellars certainly reflecting a great age (it is interesting to note that under the vicar's seat in the church is a carving of a griffin which dates from 1350). According to historical records, Gresford church was a focal point for pilgrims from the 1300s through to the 1500s. It is believed the church held an object of veneration and of important religious significance although research has not been able to confirm what this object might have been. Images within several of the windows and within other features in the church may, however, provide some clues. The east window of the Trevor chapel has two panels commemorating St Anthony. In the same window St Apollania, the patron saint of dentists, appears equipped with a large pair of pincers. The Trevor chapel was originally called St Catherine's chapel, old village records confirm that she was a favourite saint in Gresford, this being reflected in the fact that the village spring was named St Catherine's Well and many girls born in the village in the sixteenth and seventeenth centuries were baptised Catherine. In the Lady chapel, a canopied niche rests on a large carved head of the Green Man, originally a pagan god of the countryside and fertility. The niche now holds a statue of the Virgin and Child but could have been the place where the venerated figure probably stood. Could it have been an earlier effigy of the Virgin that has now been lost, or could it have been an effigy of All Hallows or All Saints, to whom the church is dedicated? It is known that a bequest was made in the will of one John Roden in 1512, that money be available "… to buy a yard and a quarter of velvet to make All Hallows a coat, and pay for the making". In spite of the true identity of the object of veneration, it is probable that the effigy played an important role in Gresford becoming a place of pilgrimage well into the mid-sixteenth century.

It is interesting to note that the earlier church of 1350 was almost completely demolished in the late fifteenth century when it was replaced by the splendid church we see today. Some historians believe that this new church, built in the Perpendicular style with all its richness of architecural features, was financed by the gifts donated by pilgrims to

Gresford. Others suggest that the church's richness is a result of the patronage of Thomas Stanley, earl of Derby, whose brother, Sir William Stanley, held the lordship and castle of nearby Holt whose chapelry, in the past, had been within the parish of Gresford. It is also known that the great east window of the church was a gift from Sir Thomas Stanley.

The beauty of the church's interior is enhanced by a feeling of light and space. The glorious camberbeam roof has panels enriched with bosses of leaves and flowers with carved stone corbels supporting the rafters. As the light falls through the windows the exquisite stained glass, which has survived over so many years, confirms once again that Gresford church benefitted from the gifts and skills of superb craftsmen. Around the church are several magnificent monumental sculptures but one of the most poignant memorials is a miner's lamp hanging on a cross, beneath this a plaque names fifteen men from the parish who died in the Gresford Colliery Disaster of 1934, when a total of 264 men lost their lives. This had a devastating effect on the village and the surrounding area, leaving 160 widows and over 200 children fatherless. On the outskirts of the village, near the Gresford Colliery Social Club, a pit-head wheel was erected and unveiled in 1982 as a memorial to the disaster victims. In 1994, a memorial painting by Dennis Bates was dedicated and installed in the Trevor Chapel, below which is a book containing the names of all those who died.

The exterior of the church, dominated by the splendid tower, has a variety of stone carvings above the windows and embattled parapets above. Even the downspouts are held by carved monkeys or grotesque creatures. The tower itself, the lower level dating from the fourteenth century with the upper level being added after 1512, has a band of carved ornamentation marking the two levels. Again carved figures and the eight pinnacles atop the tower, add to the overall impact it makes on the scene. It is this tower that houses the famous bells listed among the 'Seven Wonders of Wales'.

Unfortunately, there is no definite knowledge about the bells of the church before 1623, although it is known the church of 1350 did have a belfry entered from the inside of the church. The present belfry was

The tower of All Saints Church, Gresford. [WAW]

added in 1514, together with a new spiral staircase and entrance from an outside door at the foot of the tower. It is possible the bells in the early belfry were destroyed during the time of the Reformation and new bells were cast around 1623. Many would ask why include a peal of bells as a wonder? If the church held six bells at the time the Seven Wonders of Wales rhyme was written, their peal would have justified their being included. The author of the rhyme would have marvelled that a small village boasted such a magnificent church with its impressive peal of bells. Today, the church has eight bells. It was customary that curfew was formerly rung for ten minutes between 28 October and 14 February, this was reduced to five minutes at 6 p.m. at a later period. There was also a custom of tolling the passing bell the day before a funeral. This would last three hours for a man, two hours for a woman and one hour for a child and on the day of the funeral the bell was tolled for one hour. During the Second World War the ringing of all church bells was stopped and only to be used to warn of invasion. Today, the bells are rung regularly for church services and also every Tuesday evening, attracting teams of bell-ringers from far and wide who wish to have the pleasure of ringing the famous bells.

The village today is a vibrant community, having spread out from its original, close proximity to the church. It is around the church, however, that we see the older buildings of the village, the dame school opposite the north gate of the churchyard was built in 1725. Nearby are the almshouses built at the same time.

Not far from the church is the village pond, reflecting the cluster of surrounding houses and the church tower in the background. The pond is now home to a variety of water fowl and an attractive feature in the village. Since the construction of the A483 by-pass, the village does not have as much heavy traffic and yet still manages to support a variety of businesses and activities which meet the needs of the local community.

The journey from Gresford to the next 'wonder' takes us through the villages of Marford and Rossett. Both villages have strong historical links to the development and progress of this border area over many centuries. It has been suggested that their names are modern versions of Anglo-

Saxon names given to the agricultural settlements established here before the Norman Conquest of 1066. The 'Mar' in Marford deriving from the Anglo-Saxon word 'Maere' meaning boundary and the 'sett' in Rossett from the Anglo-Saxon word for maintained grassland or meadow. The early form of Marford was probably 'Maereford' meaning boundary ford and a ford existed where the bridge now crosses the Alyn. As for Rossett, some claim that it is not of Anglo-Saxon origin but rather from the Welsh *Yr Orsedd* meaning 'seat' or 'throne', in this case a 'Judgement seat' where the court of the old township of Marford was held. Both Marford and Rossett, together with Gresford, were placed in England after Offa built his dyke and since that time, until well into the fifteenth century, they were the victims of complex allegiances and changing boundaries. Marford, however, as a result of a dispute, found itself in isolation within a separate enclave of the old county of Flintshire where it remained until the counties were reorganised in 1974 when the old counties of Flintshire and neighbouring Denbighshire formed the new county of Clwyd. Today, it forms the northern area of Wrexham County Borough.

As the road descends down Marford Hill, the expanse of the Cheshire plain stretches out to the horizon. Over the years, several imposing houses have been built on the hill, as yet they do not impair the view. At the bottom of the hill is a cluster of houses which are unique in their structure and appearance. Built on land which was part of the Trevalyn Hall estate, between 1813–15, the cottages have what many describe as a Gothic appearance, but the true identity of the architect is not known. They were built to house workers on the Trevalyn estate, one of the larger estates in the area, with the impressive Trevalyn Hall situated below the village. In all probability, the original cottages had thatched roofs which were later replaced with slate. The overall outer appearance of the cottages has changed little over the years and their curious features of decorative crosses and oval, eye-shaped windows come as a surprise. Many theories have been put forward as to the origin of the cottages' design but as yet no acceptable theory has been confirmed. There is, however, a local legend which some believe provides the answer to why the cottages have such an unusual design. In 1713, Sir George

Marford, c.1910 – very little has changed in the last 100 years. [WAW]

Blackbourne lived in Rofft Hall in Marford. He was the steward of the lands of Marford and nearby Hoseley. Known as a harsh and cruel man, especially in the treatment of his wife, the Lady Margaret, who suffered regularly as a result of his heavy drinking. The story goes that one night, when Sir George returned home in a drunken state, Lady Margaret was waiting for him and an argument broke out between them relating to his continous bouts of drunkeness and her suspicions of his liasons with other women. The servants, awakened by the sounds of angry voices and shocked by a high-pitched scream followed by a deathly silence, dared not venture forth to see what had happened. The following morning the lifeless body of Lady Margaret was found lying at the foot of the stairs. Sir George very quickly managed to persuade everyone that his wife's death was an accident and was not prosecuted. Very soon he brought a new mistress to the hall, having married a servant girl from one of the taverns he frequented. But life was never going to be the same for Sir George and his young wife. On the night of their return, Lady Margaret's spirit rose from the grave and made its way silently through Marford village, tapping on the windows of the cottages as it progressed towards the hall. Arriving at the hall, the spirit confronted Sir George and his young wife. Sir George was unafraid but his new wife fled in terror. This ghostly walk continued over a long period until even Sir George felt he could take no more and he hired exorcists to lay Lady Margaret's spirit to rest. They were not successful and the ghost continued to haunt the village and Sir George from time to time. In the early years of the nineteenth century, Sir George Boscawen, the heir to the Trevalyn estate decided to rebuild the village of Marford. Some say that the new cottages, which we see today, were built to this unique design because the villagers were afraid that with the new construction Lady Margaret's spirit would be disturbed. To some of the villagers, living in superstitious times, the eye-shaped windows would 'see' the spirit coming from afar and so give them fair warning of its approach, whilst the crosses adorning the cottage walls would keep them safe. Whatever the reason for their unusual design, be it fact or fiction, the curious houses of Marford are well worth a visit.

Leaving Marford the road passes the impressive looking Trevalyn Hall, once the hub of a large estate owned by the Trevor family, many of whom have memorials in Gresford church. Before crossing the bridge over the river Alyn, the black and white structure of Rossett Mill can be seen on the left. This was a working mill well into the twentieth century. What we see today is a renovated building, now a private dwelling with the huge external water wheel still intact. Above the door is the date 1661, referring to the year the mill was rebuilt after a fire had destroyed the original building. In earlier times, the mill was known as upper Marford Mill and served quite a large area within the old township of Marford. A dispute arose between neighbouring landowners and the land on which Rossett Mill now stands was taken over by the lord of nearby Hope, leaving the inhabitants on the south side of the river Alyn without the services of a mill, a facility which was essential in those days for an area so highly dependent on agriculture. The lack of a mill also meant a significant loss of income for the local lord. A new mill was built on the other side of the river, practically opposite Rossett Mill, which was known as lower Marford Mill. This was rebuilt in 1791 with two new water wheels added later. Over time, this mill became derelict but was

Trevalyn Hall, Rossett. [WAW]

rescued in 1972–3 when it was converted into offices, the scheme being awarded two conservation awards. Although no longer working mills, both have a new purpose and stand to remind us of the times when land and borders in this area were in constant dispute. The journey to the next of the 'Seven Wonders' has been made easy with the construction of the A55 which is only a short distance away from Marford and Rossett along the A483.

Wonder 6
Hawarden – Northop – Holywell –
ST WINIFRED'S WELL – Basingwerk Abbey –
Whitford – St Asaph

THE A55 WAS BUILT in order to provide a fast route to and from north Wales, but tends to by-pass places which have a link with the past and an interesting tale to tell. One such place is Hawarden, only six miles from Chester, which for centuries had controlled the route into north Wales during times of conflict. Boasting two castles, Hawarden was mentioned in the Domesday Book. One castle, now a rather romantic looking ruin, was built by the Normans on the site of an earlier settlement. It was destroyed by Prince Llywelyn in 1265. During the course of rebuilding, it was attacked in 1282 by Llywelyn's brother, Dafydd, in an attempt to prevent this ancient gateway to Wales being barred by an English fortress. Although initially successful in capturing the castle, Dafydd's triumph was short lived as, following his brother's death in 1282, he was himself captured, put on trial and condemned to death by being hanged, drawn and quartered at Shrewsbury, possibly the first person to suffer this horrendous form of execution. Hawarden Castle once more became a powerful defensive feature of this border area, giving it a vital role during the English Civil War when it was besieged twice and changed hands three times, eventually to be made untenable by Cromwell's forces in 1647. Now referred to as the 'Old Castle' it stands guard over the second Hawarden Castle which was in fact a country house built in the eighteenth century, when it was known as Broadlane Hall. Between 1809–10 the owner, Sir Stephen Glynne, decided to enlarge and renovate the hall in a castellated style and renamed it Hawarden Castle. Its claim to fame lies in the fact that it became the home of William Gladstone, the

The keep at Hawarden Castle (photographed in c.1910. [WAW]

Victorian Prime Minister who came here in 1839 to be married to the castle's Welsh heiress, Catherine Glynne. For sixty years he made the place his home and it is still the private residence of his descendents. The parish church has an elaborate marble memorial to both William Gladstone and his wife. Not far from the castle is St Deiniol's library which was founded in 1895 by William Gladstone as a place of study and a centre of Christian learning. He transferred some 30,000 of his own books to a temporary building on the site. The construction of the building we see today began after Gladstone's death in 1898. Between 1899 and 1902, the library portion was built as part of the National Gladstone memorial. In front of the library is a memorial, also commissioned by the National Gladstone Memorial committee erected here in 1925. St Deiniol's library is unique in so much as it is a residential library and welcomes students and scholars from all over the world to reside here whilst researching their chosen subjects. The parish church of St Deiniol is situated near the library. Much restored over the years, it is an impressive building boasting perpendicular and decorative styles. Inside, at the east end of the north aisle is the small Gladstone memorial chapel with its monument to William Gladstone and his wife, Catherine.

Before returning to the A55 another castle at nearby Ewloe is worthy of a visit. Unlike many castles in the area, this is recognised as a native Welsh castle built, not by the Normans or Edward I, but by a Welsh prince. The original castle was probably built by Llywelyn Fawr (the Great) around 1210 and the remains of the D-shaped tower dates from this period. The castle then became the power base for Llywelyn ap Gruffydd from 1257. Recognised today as the most complete and unaltered of all native Welsh castles, it stands on a wooded promontory above steep ravines, a stone's throw away from the roar of modern day traffic on the nearby A55 and yet unseen by the thousands of motorists as they hurtle by.

A few miles west of Ewloe, just off the A55, the imposing landmark of the tower of Northop Parish Church draws attention. The Welsh name of the village is Llaneurgain, named after Eurgain, the daughter of Maelgwn Gwynedd, a sixth century Welsh prince. It is possible that a simple *llan* or church enclosure was established here in those early days. Records confirm that a church stood here in the middle of the thirteenth century and some of this building remains today.The cost of building the

Prime Minister William Gladstone and his family at Hawarden. [WAW]

present church is said to have been met by Margaret Beaufort, the mother of Henry VII. Returning to the A55, the road rises and soon the open vista of the Dee estuary can be seen with the Wirral peninsula in the far distance. On a clear day, the Liver Building and the Anglican Cathedral in Liverpool are both visible.

Sign posts soon indicate the exit off the A55 to Holywell. The town, once a busy coaching stop on the north Wales route, has also been famed for its industry and for its holy well. The busy high street is at the top of the town, with industry sited by the springs and water courses, necessary for the factories, down below in the Greenfield valley. In the second half of the eighteenth century, Holywell was an important centre for the lead-mining industry and also had numerous woollen and other mills which all depended on ample supplies of water. Holywell's industries have long since disappeared but one phenomenon remains constant, that is the Holy Well of St Winifred.

Although there are many holy wells to be seen the length and breadth of Wales, it is only St Winifred's that is recorded as one of the 'Seven Wonders of Wales'. Many wells are associated with early saints and have interesting legends and stories attached to them, together with particular healing powers. But the fame of St Winifred's Well and its ability to heal the sick and suffering over many, many centuries places it in a special category. Many consider St Winifred's Well to be a Welsh 'Lourdes', having been a place of pilgrimage since the seventh century with records of the pilgrims dating back to the twelfth century.

The well is situated on the roadside leading down from the centre of town and is surrounded by the well chapel, with the parish church of St James on the hillside above. Legend has it that Winifred (also Winefride, Winefrede and known in Welsh as Gwenffrewi) was the daughter of a local prince named Tewyth and his wife Gwenlo, who was a sister to St Beuno, a Celtic saint. Beuno had been asked by Winifred's parents to guide their young daughter towards a life of meditation and prayer. One day, Caradoc, a chieftain from nearby Hawarden, attempted to seduce Winifred and the young girl fled for safety to the nearby church built by her uncle. Unfortunately, she was unable to escape and, when Caradoc

The beautiful perpendicular buildings at St Winifrede's Well, Holywell. [WAW]

caught up with her, he cut off her head. A spring of water then gushed out of the hillside where her head had fallen to the ground. St Beuno came out of his church and taking up her head, placed it back on her body. He then prayed and Winifred was brought back to life. Caradoc sank into the ground and was never seen again. From that day Winifred bore a white scar around her neck, a sign of her martyrdom. After this amazing incident, Winifred became a nun and later joined a community of nuns at Gwytherin, a remote village above the Conwy valley, where she later became abbess. When she died, she was buried in the local churchyard but her relics were later moved to Shrewsbury Abbey in 1138.

By the Middle Ages, the legend of St Winifred, and the healing powers of the well, had spread far and wide as pilgrims made their way to Holywell. The pilgrims were from all classes of society, both rich and poor believing in the miraculous healing powers of the well. It is said that Henry V prayed to St Winifred before he went into battle at Agincourt and made a pilgrimage of thanksgiving to Holywell after visiting her shrine in Shrewsbury. The chronicler Adam of Usk (1377–1421), confirms this: 'The King, with great reverence, went on foot in pilgrimage from Shrewsbury to St Winifred's Well in North Wales'. Devotion to the saint was at its peak during this period and precious gifts were donated to the shrine, which was by this time, in the possession of nearby Basingwerk Abbey. As royal pilgrimages to the well continued, the abbey benefitted from these gifts, and the abbott in return entertained his royal guests in a most lavish fashion. It is known that many Welsh bards sang in praise of St Winifred, amongst them Tudur Aled whose *cywydd*, a poem in strict metre consisting of rhymed seven-syllable couplets, is recognised as the best known and most technically perfect. He also wrote of Edward IV's pilgrimage to the well; after paying his devotions, the king placed some of the soil from near the well on his crown. Even Richard III (1483–85), desperate to preserve his crown, made a donation to the abbott of Basingwerk to support a priest at the chapel of St Winifred. It is not surprising that one of the chief benefactors who contributed generously towards the building of the chapel well was the pious Lady Margaret Beaufort, countess of Richmond and Derby, wife of Thomas Stanley and mother of King Henry VII. Her patronage was extensive, for the churches at Northop, Gresford, Holt and Mold (and possibly Wrexham) also benefitted from her generosity.

By the end of the fifteenth century, the chapel well building was completed, its fine perpendicular arches rising gracefully over the waters below. The fan vaulting over the well is quite splendid and where they meet, a carved pendant projection depicts six scenes from the life of St Winifred. The well chamber actually lies below the aisle and to the east of the chapel nave. Records reveal that it was customary for pilgrims to pass through the water three times. This was associated with St Winifred's prayer, written down in the twelfth century by the prior of Shrewsbury as encouragement for all who prayed at the well: '... that they might receive an answer to their request at least at the third time'. It is likely, however, that the custom is very ancient, deriving from the Celtic ritual of triple immersion. An interesting carving, that almost overlooks the bathing part of the well, shows a pilgrim carrying another on his back, suggesting that it was the custom then, just as it is now, to carry sick pilgrims through the water. The chapel has many decorative carvings, several of them emblems of the benefactors of the chapel, in particular the Stanley family. Other carvings are of real and mythical creatures, all displaying the skill and, in some examples, the humour of the medieval craftsmen.

The well is approached by a series of bathing pools through which the pilgrims pass before immersing themselves in the well. Near the steps, on one of these outer pools is a stone called St Beuno's stone where the saint supposedly sat when instructing St Winifred. After going through the inner well three times, it is customary for pilgrims to kneel on this stone and complete their prayers. From the time of its building until the Dissolution of the Monastries, the well and its chapel were the focal point for the gathering of pilgrims from far and wide. The Cistercian monks of Basingwerk Abbey were always ready to offer Mass and preached in the chapel, particularly on St Winifred's Day. This was all suddenly disrupted when the abbey was dissolved and the well chapel taken over by Henry VIII's servants. Because the offerings made at the well were so valuable, the chapel was not destroyed, but leased to one William Holcroft who was responsible for collecting the offerings and sending them to the King.

In spite of the Reformation, pilgrims continued to flock to St Winifred's Well, but there was persistent conflict over its ownership. With the brief reign of Queen Mary (1553–8), the Roman Catholic bishop of St Asaph was able to install a priest to care for the well and its chapel once more. But the long drawn out struggle between Protestant and Catholic was soon re-kindled, although pilgrims continued to visit the well, they were under close scrutiny at all times. During the English Civil War, the chapel and the well were badly damaged and the statue of St Winifred, resting in its niche near the well, was destroyed. When the Catholic King James II and his wife Queen Mary of Modena announced in 1686 that they wished to visit the well in order 'to crave the prayers of St Winifred that they might be blessed with a son,' it caused great consternation because the well and chapel were in such a bad state of repair. As a token of thanksgiving, the king presented part of a dress worn by the Catholic Mary, Queen of Scots at her execution, to the chapel and his wife gave £30 towards repair of the well and chapel building. This visit also resulted in the local Jesuits being given possession of the chapel and some essential repairs being carried out on the building. A stone marking James and Mary's pilgrimage can be seen on the side of the well basin. In 1688, when the Queen gave birth to a son it was thought St Winifred's prayers had answered the king and queen's plea. Protestants, however, were not happy at the thought of a Catholic heir threatening the throne and this triggered a violent reaction resulting in the Jesuits losing possession of the chapel well of St Winifred. Pilgrims, however, continued to visit in the face of severe opposition until the Protestants finally took it over completely in 1723 converting it into a school room. It seemed that this was the end of a long and courageuos struggle to preserve the chapel for Catholic use.

Until the end of the eighteenth century, and even into the early nineteenth century, the legend of St Winifred, and the presence of her shrine and well in Holywell, continued to draw pilgrims but not in such large numbers. Towards the end of the nineteenth century, however, there was a steady increase as Catholicism gradually came out of the persecution which had begun with the Reformation. The Sisters of Charity settled in Holywell in 1859, establishing a convent some years later. At nearby Pantasaph, more nuns and friars created a flourishing community to provide hospitality and spiritual support to the ever increasing numbers of visiting pilgrims to St Winifred's Well and by the turn of the twentieth century, Holywell was bustling once more during the summer months '… crowded with zealous pilgrims from all parts of Britain'. It could be said, therefore, that pilgrimage to the well never really died out, even during the difficult times and it is the only shrine in Britain able to make this claim. Now the well is officially in the care of the Roman Catholic Church.

Further buildings have been built in Well Street over the years, such as St Winifred's Roman Catholic Church, which was extended in 1909. The Well Garden was also established in 1930 on the site of the old St Winifred's Mill and Brewery, together with a house for the custodian of the well. On the day of St Winifred's Feast, the well chapel and garden is usually full to overflowing for the outdoor mass. There is no doubt that St Winifred's Well as a fully operational working shrine, remains a rarity, not only in Wales, but in Britain as a whole. Today's pilgrims are allowed to bathe in its waters at set times on weekday mornings.

The amount of water coming from the well was originally much greater than it is now. When Dr Johnson visited the town and the well he noted that '… it yields a 100 tuns of water in a minute and all at once becomes a great stream … turning a mill within 30 yards of its eruption and in the course of 2 miles 18 mills more.' In 1917, however, Holywell was devastated when mining operations at nearby Halkyn cut through the underground stream which flowed into the well, causing it to be diverted. Much to the despair of the town and the pilgrims, the well went completely dry. This also affected the mills which had relied on a steady flow of water and resulted in great hardship for the workforce. Eventually, to the wonderment of many, another spring of water erupted naturally a short distance away from the original source. This was diverted and the waters flowed once again into the well and the mills below.

Before leaving St Winifred's Well a visit should be made to the parish church of St James perched on the hillside above the well. It was founded by St Beuno in the seventh century before he moved to Clynnog Fawr in Gwynedd, where he built a church and established a convent. St Beuno ranks highly amongst Welsh saints, regarded by some to be second only to St David. It was when visiting his relatives in north-east Wales that he was gifted a piece of land by his brother-in-law, the father of St Winifred. He established his church on this land and took his niece Winifred into his care, guiding her to a life of prayer and meditation. The present church is the result of re-building in the eighteenth century with only the tower remaining from the fourteenth century, later restored and modernised in 1884–5. Inside the church are a number of old objects of interest, one in particular being the small hand bell mentioned by Thomas Pennant in his book *A Tour of Wales*. It seems that because the church is so tucked under the hillside that the peal of bells from its tower could not be heard in the town above and a bell ringer was appointed who went around the town ringing the hand bell, calling the people to worship. In the process of ringing the bell it seems the swinging arm movement often caused the bell-ringer to strike his knee with the bell and a protective leather knee pad was made for him which is also preserved in the church. A knee pad then became an essential part of a bell-ringer's apparel in other parishes. The bell ringer was also given the additional responsibility of walking ahead of funeral processions, ringing his hand bell in order to give a clear warning to road users on the narrow, twisty roads which existed in the area. This was a tradition in many rural areas and it remained so in Holywell until 1857.

A mile to the west of Holywell, in Pantasaph, a Franciscan friary was founded in 1858. The church of St David, which adjoins the friary, had been built in 1846 by the then Viscount Fielding and Lady Louisa Pennant, great grand-daughter of Thomas Pennant, as a thanksgiving for their marriage. Originally intended to be part of the Established Church, this changed when the donors converted to Roman Catholicism in 1850.

The copper works in the Greenfield Valley depicted in an eighteenth-century print. [WAW]

The bishop of St Asaph attempted to oppose this but failed and the church was given a more 'Catholic finish' by the architect Pugin. The Franciscan community was established in 1852, once again under the auspices of Viscount Fielding and his wife, who later became the earl and countess of Denbigh. On a hillside behind the friary is a set of the Stations of the Cross dating from 1875. Below its summit of the hillside is a small chapel and above this a calvary, with a cross of iron and figures in bronze. This place continues to serve as a peaceful retreat to many today, away from the hustle and bustle of modern-day living.

Returning to Holywell and descending down the hill from the Parish Church and St Winifred's Well, the road leads to Greenfield which played a vital role in the development of industries in the area during the the the Industrial Revolution. As the industries grew, so did the population of Holywell, making it the biggest town in the county of Flint by the 1880s. A continuous line of factories and mills occupied the hillside from St Winifred's Well to the docks at Greenfield on the Dee estuary. Houses were built for the workers and the area hummed with the sound of machinery. It is amazing that such a variety of industries were working in such a relatively small area – weaving mills spinning the cotton that came from America and the rolling mills shaping copper from Parys Mountain in Anglesey into pots and pans, before being shipped out to Africa from the port of Liverpool. Thomas Pennant refers to the prosperity that these new industries brought to the area and of the great number of people who benefitted from employment. The original source of power for the industries came from the same source as that of the Holy Well, descending into a series of factory pools and it can be said that Holywell nurtured religion and industry side by side. Many of the old industries have now disappeared leaving only remnants of buildings and machinery. Fortunately, a Heritage Park has been established in Greenfield, featuring ancient monuments and examples of industrial history where visitors can experience what it was like to live in those vibrant times of religious fervour and industrial development.

A waymarked path leads from St Winifred's Well through the park to the picturesque ruins of Basingwerk Abbey. The abbey was originally founded in 1132 on another site, transferring to this site in 1157 and becoming affiliated to the Cistercian order. Basingwerk became renowned for its hospitality in welcoming pilgrims visiting the shrine of St Winifred which provided the abbey with a steady, additional income from the offerings of the pilgrims, making it a very prosperous monastery. Because of its close proximity to the coastal route from Chester into north Wales, it also welcomed other travellers such as Gerald Cambrensis (Gerald of Wales) who visited the abbey in 1188. Unfortunately, Henry VIII's Dissolution of the Monasteries saw Basingwerk stripped of its rich fittings. The ruins which remain date from the early thirteenth century and were originally the monastic church, the cloisters, the chapter house and the novices' lodging with a dormitory above. Adjacent to this is the most impressive ruin of the thirteenth century dining refectory or *frater*. Here it is possible to make out the 'reader's pulpit' where the reader would read to the diners in the hope of improving their minds whilst their palates were being stimulated by food and wine. So great was the hospitality at Basingwerk that two successive meal sittings had to be arranged as the refectory was not big enough for all the monks, visitors and pilgrims to dine at the same time. The nearby farm was able to provide the abbey with most of its food, with the nearby woods and moorland providing meat and game in the form of venison, pheasant, hare and rabbit.

A few miles along the coast road from Greenfield, the docks at Mostyn have been re-developed in recent years in the hope that it will once again become the busy port it was in the past. It is not known when the port was originally established but records show it certainly existed during the time of the English Civil War. Tradition has it that the earl of Richmond, who later became King Henry VII, narrowly missed being captured by the troops of Richard III in nearby Mostyn Hall. When the soldiers forced their way into the hall they found an extra place set at the table confirming their suspicions that the earl was a guest there. Lord Mostyn, however, reassured them that it was customary to lay an extra place at the table for an unexpected visitor. Whilst this delaying tactic was being played out, the earl is reputed to have made his escape through a

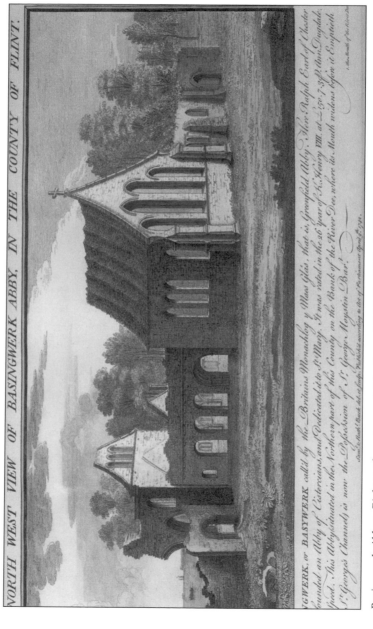

Basingwerk Abbey. Eighteenth-century print by Samuel & Nathaniel Buck. [WAW]

window, fleeing to the port below from where he safely sailed away. A fine tale but one that is not borne out by any historical evidence.

The north Wales coast has a history of smuggling and during the reign of William III the stretch of coast at Mostyn was rife with the smuggling of tobacco, wines and French linen, much of it being instigated by the local gentry. The customs officials fought a never-ending battle in an attempt to catch the smugglers but their efforts were often foiled. A raid in Mostyn in 1702 is said to have recovered a large quantity of French wine which was taken to a local inn for safe-keeping overnight. According to Thomas Pennant, the inn was raided, the customs men tied up and the wine taken. It was thought the raid was carried out by local miners but many claim it was the work of the local gentry, headed by the Mostyn family, who held most of land from Flint along the coast as far as Llandudno.

The inn in question related to this particular story is 'The Honest Man' which still stands on the A548 in Mostyn. Its unusual name is reflected in its unusual inn sign above the door – the figure of a man's head and a sheep. One story tells of a local man who stole a sheep, but before killing it, he realised it was a hanging offence. So overcome with guilt and the thought of a possible sentence, he returned the sheep to its owner. His action made him an honest man in the eyes of the local community and this is one explanation of how the inn got its name. Another story however, tells of one of the inn's licensees, a man who always cleared his debts and paid cash for everything he bought, a truly 'honest man'! In spite of these tales of honesty, the actions of some of its locals could not be considered altogether honest for the inn in fact, sits on underground tunnels, one running down to the old port of Mostyn and the other running up to the Mostyn estate. These tunnels were a quick route for smugglers to bring in their goods from the ships docked in Mostyn. Over time, the tunnels have deteriorated, so much so that they are now boarded up for safety reasons.

The Dee estuary at one time was a very busy and important area for shipping coming in to north Wales, having twenty-six wharves stretching from Chester to the Point of Air colliery. Over the years however, only

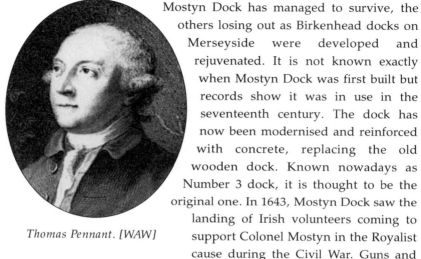

Thomas Pennant. [WAW]

Mostyn Dock has managed to survive, the others losing out as Birkenhead docks on Merseyside were developed and rejuvenated. It is not known exactly when Mostyn Dock was first built but records show it was in use in the seventeenth century. The dock has now been modernised and reinforced with concrete, replacing the old wooden dock. Known nowadays as Number 3 dock, it is thought to be the original one. In 1643, Mostyn Dock saw the landing of Irish volunteers coming to support Colonel Mostyn in the Royalist cause during the Civil War. Guns and ammunition were also smuggled through here during this time of conflict.

Mostyn Dock extended its docking facilities in recent years to offer roll-on/roll-off ferries for Ireland. Unfortunately, this did not develop as the port authority had initally hoped for, so this facility was halted, but the port is busy with its current trade of scrap metal to Spain, wood pulp and timber from Sweden and shipping out steel from the Shotton steel mills. It is quite amazing that this port, the only surviving and active port on the Dee, still has the excise and customs office which has been there since the time of the Civil War.

The coast road from Mostyn passes through several small villages with the open expanse of the Dee estuary providing panoramic views of the Wirral peninsula. The estuary is also a vital and important area for migrating birds, plant and animal life with stretches of it protected by the R.S.P.B. and the Environment Agency. It was whilst travelling with his father, from his home above the coast, that the young Emlyn Williams, the Welsh actor and dramatist, wondered at the panorama of river estuary and distant shores that opened up as they descended into Mostyn. Looking across the estuary towards Parkgate on the Wirral, he

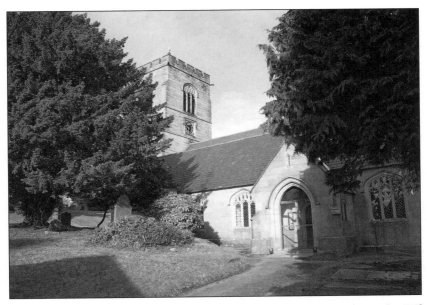

The parish church at Whitford. [WAW]

asked his father the name of the land he could see on the horizon with all that sand. His father's answer and his own reaction is recorded in Williams' autobiography *George* (1961) – 'He said it was another country, where Welsh was not spoken and the public-houses were open on a Sunday. I remembered the Sahara, and asked if it was Africa? He laughed and said it was, and that on a clear day you could see elephants walking in and out of Parkgate.'

The countryside above the coast road is full of interest and history and has nurtured several other notable Welshmen. The area is criss-crossed with narrow roads linking rural communities and small villages such as Trelogan, the birth-place and home of David Lloyd the well-known Welsh tenor. Thomas Pennant, the intrepid eighteenth-century traveller and antiquarian, was born just outside the village of Whitford in Downing, the family's home set in extensive grounds. Built in 1627 the house was demolished following a fire in 1922. Pennant was descended from an old Welsh family which had owned the neighbouring estate of

Bychton since the twelfth century. Referred to by Dr Johnson as '... the best traveller I have read,' Pennant's book, *Tours in Wales*, remains the classic of all the older books on Welsh travel. In H.L.V. Fletcher's book, *The Queen's Wales, North Wales*, Pennant is described as '... an observer, shrewd, accurate and kindly, and, considering his travels were all made on horseback, it is remarkable what very little ground he left uncovered.' There is no doubt that his knowledge of the Welsh language, his sympathy for the ordinary people and his love for the country resulted in his producing a book which gives an accurate picture of Wales as it was before the Industrial Revolution. A memorial to Thomas Pennant can be seen inside the parish church of St Mary's, Whitford. Rebuilt in 1843–46 its interior retains its seventeenth century font and has several thirteenth and fourteenth sepulchral slabs. Outside, against the north wall of the churchyard, is the tomb-chest of Moses Griffiths, one of Pennant's travelling companions and the illustrator of his books. The church lychgate is unusual in that it has a room over it, probably dating from the seventeenth century.

A short distance west of Whitford stands 'Maen Achwyfan' a monolithic slab cross of the late tenth or early eleventh century. Intricately carved on all sides with Celtic motifs, together with carved interlaced chain patterns of Scandinavian influence, it is regarded as one of the finest examples of a wheel cross to be found in Wales. There has been much speculation over the centuries as to the origins of the name of this cross. Some say it is named after St Cwyfan, an early Celtic saint, others claim it is a lamentation stone on the Holywell pilgrimage route. From Whitford the road meanders through well-wooded countryside eventually re-joining the busy A55. As St Winifred's Well, together with other buildings and communities linked to it, have had such an influence on the religious life of this area, it seems a visit to St Asaph's cathedral is appropriate before heading towards the seventh wonder of Snowdon.

Situated in a prominent position above the episcopal city of St Asaph, the cathedral is said to be the smallest in Wales and England. It is fair to say, however, that its smallness of size does not detract from its dignity of appearance. Dr Johnson said that it '... has something of dignity and grandeur.' Founded in the sixth century by Kentigern, a Celtic saint who came to this area from Scotland, as a church it gradually grew into a thriving monastery. Kentigern later returned to Scotland leaving his favourite disciple, Asa, as his successor. It was Asa, also later to became a saint, who gave his name to the town, St Asaph, and to the nearby villages of Pantasaph and Llanasa also within the bishopric of St Asaph. An old legend recounts how Queen Nest, the beautiful wife of Maelgwn Gwynedd, the sixth century king of Gwynedd, lost a precious ring whilst she was bathing in the river Elwy beside her home in St Asaph. Fearing the wrath of her husband over the loss of the ring, which had been handed down over generations to be worn by the queens of the north, Nest ran to Bishop Asa to seek his help and support in breaking the news to her husband. Whilst dining with the couple that evening, the bishop tactfully revealed to Maelgwn what had happened and was able to curb and subdue the king's anger towards his wife. After offering a prayer, the three continued with their meal. It was whilst Asa was serving Nest a portion of salmon that, to their astonishment, the sacred ring fell onto her plate from where it had been embedded in the fish's flesh. Once again

The cathedral church of St Asaph. [WAW]

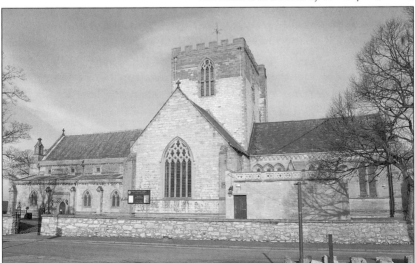

the ring, having travelled full circle – from finger to river to salmon was back home on Nest's finger.

After Asa's death, around AD 597, records relating to the church and the monastery are very sparse. What is known, however, is that the original wooden buildings were replaced by others of stone. It is also known that the bishopric of St Asaph was terminated for a period of time and was not re-established until 1143 as part of the Norman re-organisation of the Welsh Church. From 1152 to his death in 1154 Geoffrey of Monmouth, noted for his *History of the Kings of Britain*, was bishop. In 1188, Geraldus Cambrensis accompanied Baldwin, archbishop of Canterbury, on a crusading mission in north Wales and whilst staying at Rhuddlan Castle visited St Asaph Cathedral where Baldwin celebrated Mass. As a result of conflict between King Edward I and Bishop Anian II the cathedral was burnt down by English soldiers and Edward planned to transfer the bishopric from St Asaph to Rhuddlan, the new borough he had created. Strong opposition and local tradition foiled his scheme and the reconstruction of the cathedral probably commenced in 1284 and continued until 1381, the tower being completed in 1382. Unfortunately, in 1402, the cathedral was once again burnt during the time of Owain Glyndŵr, his soldiers undoing the work of nearly a century. Rebuilding was not completed until well into the fifteenth century.

The turmoil of the English Civil War saw the cathedral once again under threat and repairs and renovation continued until a major restoration was undertaken by Sir Gilbert Scott in the period 1867–75. The cathedral interior does not have the spatial splendour of other episcopal churches but has an overall effect described as consistent, harmonious and austere. Its choir stalls, however, dating from the late fifteenth century are highly decorative and are the only remaining medieval canopied stalls in Wales. Here and there traces of older building can be seen where a variety of stone is visible in the walls.

The vestry houses a number of interesting articles such as a copy of a Breeches Bible, old Welsh Bibles and prayer books, a first edition of the Authorised Version of the Bible and several old manuscripts. Of particular interest is the manuscript of a Hebrew–Greek–Welsh dictionary compiled by Dic Aberdaron. Born Richard Jones in Aberdaron in 1780, Dic grew up to be a skilled linguist, being fluent in many languages. He spent his life wandering through Wales and England, always poor and with the appearance of a vagrant, he was dependant upon patrons to support him. He spent a great deal of time in Liverpool, where he would be seen wandering the streets carrying many books and usually a harp. He died in St Asaph in 1843 where he had lived for a few months and is buried in the parish church of St Kentigern.

The Translators' Memorial, St Asaph, showing Bishop William Morgan and Dean Gabriel Goodman. [WAW]

Outside the cathedral, in the churchyard, facing the High Street, is the Translators' Memorial, commemorating the tercentenary of Bishop William Morgan's Welsh Bible of 1588. The city of St Asaph clings to the side of the hillside leading down to the river Elwy below which gives the it its Welsh name of Llanelwy.

Crossing the bridge, the roadsigns direct the traveller very quickly to the busy A55 from where a scenic route will lead to the seventh and final wonder – 'Snowdon Mountain without its people'.

Wonder 7

Bodelwyddan – Abergele – Elwy Valley – Llanrwst – Betws-y-Coed – Capel Curig – SNOWDON'S MOUNTAIN

THE JOURNEY FROM THE SIXTH TO THE SEVENTH WONDER can follow a variety of routes. The coastal route takes in the busy coastal towns with their constantly changing seascapes. A more leisurely route moves further inland, through small villages surrounded by wooded hills and moorland. This latter route is the one chosen to take us into the majestic scenery of Snowdonia.

On leaving St Asaph, heading westwards along the A55 North Wales Expressway, the gleaming white spire of Bodelwyddan Church rises gracefully beside the busy road. Built in 1856–80, at the expense of Lady Margaret de Willoughby, in memory of her husband, it is known as the 'Marble Church' and attracts many visitors. The church's exterior is of gleaming white limestone, with its interior richly decorated with marble. Intricate carving in stone and wood confirms that only the best artist-craftsmen and materials were used. It has a unique font formed out of Carrara white marble, depicting two of Lady Margaret's nieces holding a giant scallop shell. The pulpit, supported by five kneeling angels together with the lectern, an eagle perched on a timber crag decorated with flowers, have to be seen to be believed. The church also boasts a marvellous hammer-beam roof and the stained-glass windows are quite beautiful. It is obvious that Lady Margaret decreed that no expense be spared in the building of her church.

Outside the church, in the neat lawned cemetery, are rows of graves each mounted with identical gravestones. They are the graves of

Canadian soldiers who died from the terrible Spanish influenza in nearby Kinmel Park military camp, where they were based after the end of the First World War. Bodelwyddan Castle which stands in rolling parkland opposite the church was re-modelled and extended during the nineteenth century around an Elizabethan or early seventeenth century house. Now a luxury hotel, it was for many years prior to this, a private school. In addition to the hotel facilities, the castle also houses a collection of some two hundred paintings on permanent loan from the National Portrait Gallery in London.

The market town of Abergele, named after the river Gele which runs through it, is now by-passed by the A55 but still remains a busy, bustling centre for nearby rural communities. It is interesting to note that Abergele was at one time further from the sea than at present. Old maps indicate that a wide stretch of fertile land separated the sea from the land but over time, as the coast was eroded, so the sea has encroached inland. This is further supported by a tablet in the church yard wall with a Welsh inscription, which translates into English as: 'In this churchyard lies a man who lived three miles to the north of it.' Thomas Pennant, when

Bodelwyddan Castle. [WAW]

The 'Marble Church' Bodelwyddan. [WAW]

travelling through the area, was intrigued by this and when standing on the shore and looking out to sea '... saw bodies of oak trees, tolerably entire, but so soft as to be cut by a knife as easily as wax.' The church of St Michael is a very good example of a perpendicular double-naved church and stands on the site of a *clas* or Celtic monastery. The main structure of the present church dates from the time of Henry VIII and was sympathetically restored in 1879. The church was used as a school in Tudor times and carvings of initials and dates on the screen are said to have been made by the pupils. Other markings on the pillars were made by archers who used the pillars to sharpen their arrows.

The A548 road leads out of the centre of Abergele, passing the old Bull Hotel on the left, which has strong connections to Mormonism. Records show some of the inhabitants of Abergele and surrounding villages were amongst the first in Wales to convert to the Mormon cause. It is also believed that Brigham Young spent time in the town as a missionary of the Church of Jesus Christ of Latterday Saints. The number of converts in and around Abergele grew to such an extent that an annexe was built onto the Bull Hotel and it was registered as a place of worship in 1849. Many converts emigrated to the state of Utah, where the Mormons had established themselves in great numbers. They sailed from Liverpool and many of them became prominent members of the church in Utah. In the summer of 1990, a party of Mormons from Utah toured Wales to visit places that their ancestors had left almost a hundred and fity years before. Their visit also celebrated the first arrival of Mormon missionaries in Wales in 1840. During their visit to Abergele, the group unveiled a plaque in the dining room of the Bull Hotel which reads:

> The Church of Jesus Christ of Latterday Saints (Mormon) was begun in the state of New York in the United States. In 1837, missionaries began to proselytize in Great Britain and in 1840, the message of Mormonism was first proclaimed in Wales. The latter part of 1848 John Parry Jnr, a convert from Newmarket began to preach in the home of Jane Roberts, Crown Street, in the town of Abergele. Jane Roberts, Jane Parry, Elias Morris and Barbara Morris were the first fruits of his labours and over the years, a number of others in and around the area of Abergele converted to Mormonism and were baptized. On April 30, 1849, this appendage to the

Bull Inn was registered by Elias Morris as a place of Worship for the Abergele Branch of the LDS Church. Its use by the Mormons discontinued in April 1856 after most of the members of the Church in Abergele had emigrated to Salt Lake city in the Rocky Mountains. In this sesquicentennial year of Mormonism in Wales, the descendants of John Parry Jnr, and Elias Morris, place this plaque in memory of their ancestors and other early converts in Abergele (July 13th, 1990)

COFFA DA AMDANYNT

Soon the road is meandering through countryside dotted with large farms, interspersed with wooded hillsides and green pastures. The small village of Llanfair Talhaearn clings to the steep banks above the river Elwy. Although considered to be one of Wales' minor rivers, it is a magnet for anglers who come to fish its sparkling waters. Crossing the old stone bridge, a narrow street between the Black Lion and the old National School, terminates in an attractive village square. Here the Swan Inn has as its neighbour the old parish church of St Mary, perched on the hill above the square. Much of the church was rebuilt in 1876 but there are some traces of the medieval church still to be seen in the arched-braced roofs. The roots of this church, however, go far back in time to the sixth century when St Talhaearn settled down as a hermit in this place. Inside the church, below a disused font, is a tank now under trap doors, constructed in 1841 for adult baptism by total immersion. Last used in 1933, it once again links this place with the past and perpetuated a custom common within the early Celtic church. The church belfry boasts a weather vane in the shape of a fish, a sign perhaps, that the waters of the river below will give up ample catches to the enthusiastic anglers.

In the churchyard is the grave of John Jones, a native of the village, born in 1810 in the old Harp Inn, now a private house. He became an apprentice architect, a career which took him to London and France working on different projects but, eventually, health problems caused him to return to his home village. A man of many talents, he is best remembered throughout Wales as a poet, taking up the bardic name of 'Talhaiarn'. Sadly he took his own life in 1870.

On the opposite side of the river, hidden in the trees is Garthewin

Hall, the home of the Wynne family for over three hundred years, from when Robert Wynne married Margaret Price, the Garthewin heiress, in the seventeenth century. The house was rebuilt in the early eighteenth century with additional work being carried out in later years. Although the family had strong links with the area, these links took on a new aspect when Robert Wynne, the owner, converted an old barn near the house, into a theatre in 1938. The barn, spanned by two impressive arches, adapted well and became a prominent centre for Welsh drama, in particular the works of Saunders Lewis. In the mid 1940s, his plays were perfomed by Garthewin's own theatre company. In 1947 a drama festival was established which continued as an annual feature of the Welsh drama scene until 1968. There is no doubt that Robert Wynne and Garthewin made a major contribution to the acceptance and development of drama in Wales.

From Llanfair Talhaearn, the road passes through a wooded valley with glimpses of the river Elwy flowing through green meadows, soon entering the small, compact village of Llangernyw. Surrounded by gentle, rolling hills with their scattering of farms, one feels that this is a place very dependent on the land and its offerings. Records show that in the past, five livestock markets were held in Llangernyw every year, confirming it as the centre of a rich, agricultural community. It is said that if the number of animals to be sold was too large, they would overspill into the churchyard, and in 1749, the church porch was used by butchers to hang and sell their meat. The church is dedicated to St Digain, a sixth century Celtic saint whose father was Cystenin of Gernow, which is Cornish for *Cernyw* (Cornwall). It seems the church is named after the son, whilst the father gave his name to the village. The church is unusual in so much that it is a cruciform rather than a double-naved church, which is the most common type found in this area of north Wales. It is quite possible that the original, early church was a simple, single chamber and that the late medieval additions transformed it into the enlarged cruciform church we see today. Perched on a high bank above the river, its outer walls have recently been whitewashed giving it, once again, the appearance it had in earlier times. The lych gate is well proportioned and has the date 1745 on its lintel. The church has some features remaining from the earlier church, such as the arch-braced roof, the Perpendicular east window and the south doorway which now gives access to the vestry. One of the stained-glass windows commemorates the wife of H. R. Sandbach who lived in nearby Hafodunos Hall. A monument inside the church commemorates his father and mother, Samuel and Elizabeth Sandbach. Of great interest in the church yard is an ancient yew tree, confirmed by the Tree Council in 1995, to be 5,000 years old and the oldest and largest yew tree in Wales and England. Also in the churchyard are two pillar stones, dating from between the seventh and ninth centuries, each having a Maltese-style cross carved into the stone. Standing out amongst the gravestones is the mausoleum to the Sandbach family who came to Hafodunos Hall in 1831 having been bought by Samuel Sandbach, a wealthy Liverpool merchant and shipowner. The family maintained a close association with the village over many generations until the hall was sold in the late 1980s. Some features of the hall dated back to medieval times suggesting that an earlier dwelling stood here. Its name 'Hafodunos' – 'house of one night' is a name more usually associated with the temporary dwellings of herdsmen, moving their stock from the valley pastures up to the moorland pastures for the summer. When a larger, grander house was built here, it is quite likely that it took on the old name. Records do show, however, that a monastery was once sited here with, in all probability, a rest house for pilgrims to stay overnight perhaps on their way to nearby Gwytherin where St Winifrede was originally buried. This would also support the origins of the name 'Hafodunos'. Tragically, the house was destroyed by arsonists in December 2005.

Situated in the village of Llangernyw is the birthplace and childhood home of Sir Henry Jones who became one of the most brilliant of Welsh scholars. Born in 1852, the son of the village shoemaker, in a small thatched cottage on the outskirts of the village, the family later moved to a cottage in the village which is now a museum to his life. Leaving school at the age of twelve, he became an apprentice to his father. Although he became a skilled shoemaker, his ambition was to extend his education

The birthplace of Sir Henry Jones. [WAW]

further to which end, despite the long working hours in the cottage's workshop, he would continue with his studies late into the night, encouraged by the local schoolmaster, John Price, regarded as one of the best schoolmasters of his time. Henry's efforts were justly rewarded when he was accepted to train as a teacher and taught for a period of time in south Wales. He continued with his studies, eventually winning a scholarship in 1875 to Glasgow University. Here, he studied philosphy, graduating with a first-class honours degree in 1878. He spent further time studying in Germany and Oxford before eventually becoming Professor of Philosophy at Aberystwyth University and later Bangor University. In 1891, however, Henry Jones returned to Scotland to become Professor of Philosophy at St Andrew's University from where he was appointed Professor of Moral Philosophy at Glasgow University, becoming a well-known and highly regarded academic. He was also acclaimed as a fluent and inspiring lecturer on social affairs and liberalism, but he never forgot his own humble origins, and worked hard to improve the system of education in Wales. He died in 1922, the year he was made a Companion of Honour, having been knighted in 1912. Although he is buried near Glasgow, the village of Llangernyw has not

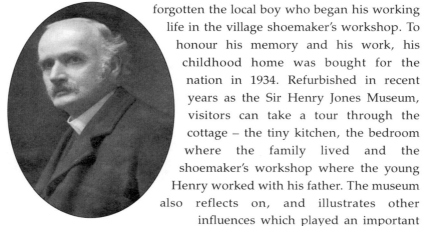

Sir Henry Jones, CH. [WAW]

forgotten the local boy who began his working life in the village shoemaker's workshop. To honour his memory and his work, his childhood home was bought for the nation in 1934. Refurbished in recent years as the Sir Henry Jones Museum, visitors can take a tour through the cottage – the tiny kitchen, the bedroom where the family lived and the shoemaker's workshop where the young Henry worked with his father. The museum also reflects on, and illustrates other influences which played an important part in young Henry's life, such as the chapel, the school and the close-knit community of this rural community.

The road from Llangernyw to Llanrwst becomes more scenic as the summits of the mountains of Snowdonia can be seen on the horizon, rising above and beyond the Conwy valley. The mountains stretch from the coast, their outlines etched against the skyline from Tal-y-Fan, above Conwy, to Carnedd Llywelyn, Carnedd Dafydd, the Glyders, each one a sentinel, as it were, guarding the approach to Yr Wyddfa – Snowdon. On a clear day, no matter which season, the scene is quite breathtaking, so many mountains, it seems in such a small space. The farms in this area are now true hill-farms, surrounded by a mixture of enclosed pastures and open moorland. A turnpike cottage on the roadside is a reminder of the days of toll-gates and the riots associated with them. Small minor roads lead off the A548 to remote, isolated communities such as Pandy Tudur and Gwytherin, each one an interesting example of a Welsh upland village before the road gradually drops down through the small hamlet of Tafarn-y-Fedw (which means the 'tavern midst the birch'). During one of the Methodist revivals in the area, the tavern was replaced by a chapel, fortunately its pretty Welsh name remained.

Soon the road enters Llanrwst, sitting on the banks of the river

Conwy, which has had an interesting and sometimes turbulent past. A battle was fought here in the tenth century when the rivalry between the Welsh princes of north and south Wales resulted in their trying to gain lands from each other. In the early fifteenth century, when Owain Glyndŵr led the Welsh in their fight to regain their independence, Llanrwst was once again the scene of bitter fighting, and in 1468 the town was completely devastated by the forces of Edward IV who stormed the valley and the town. Finally, in the seventeenth century, the English Civil War brought further conflict when the Parliamentarians sought to overcome the Royalist supporters who were very strong in the valley.

The town's position, on the banks of the river may have been a factor in its involvement in these territorial and military struggles. Being midway between the mouth of the river at Conwy and the mountains of Snowdonia, the steep wooded slopes surrounding the town provided shelter for those who sought to escape the enemy, be they rival Welsh princes or English soldiers enforcing the commands of their king. When survival was threatened, the nearby mountains, to the west of the town, provided safer refuge. In many ways Llanrwst was a 'frontier' town. There is an old Welsh saying, *Cymru, Lloegr a Llanrwst* (Wales, England and Llanrwst) which originates, it is said, from those early days when the town's inhabitants set themselves above any imposed laws, remaining independent and a law unto themselves. In spite of this, Llanrwst flourished as a market town, its position making it the focal point for the farming communities in the valley and the hills and moorlands above. By the eighteenth century, it was the eighth-largest town in Wales and became well-known for its woollen goods such as hard-wearing tweeds, knitted stockings and flannel. A variety of ales were produced in the brewery, whilst the tannery produced good quality leather. Skilled carpenters produced furniture using wood from the extensive oak woodlands in the valley. In the early eighteenth century they were producing oak Welsh dressers to a particular design, now referred to as the 'Dyffryn Conwy Welsh Dresser,' much sought after by collectors. The town also became famous for its harp-making as early as the mid sixteenth century and it is claimed that the first triple harp was made in

Llanrwst Bridge. [WAW]

Llanrwst. The town has recently revived its links with harp-making and harpists by establishing an annual harp festival. Llanrwst also had a long-established tradition of clock making, specialising in the making of longcase clocks. Records show that between 1700 and 1900, there were around twenty or more skilled clockmakers working in the town. Unfortunately, mass production took over, but there still remains in many Welsh homes a longcase clock bearing the name of one of the Owen family of Llanrwst on its dial.

The town's church is dedicated to St Grwst, a sixth-century saint who also gave his name to the town. Although the building has been much restored, there remain many features dating back to the church of 1470, but it is probable that a single-nave thatched-roof church was built here in 1170. The present church tower and north aisle date from the nineteenth century. Inside, there is an intricately carved oak rood screen said to have been taken from nearby Maenan Abbey by the Wynn's of Gwydir Castle after the Dissolution of the Monasteries. The Gwydir Chapel was added to the church by Sir Richard Wynn of Gwydir in 1633–4. There are many memorials to different members of the Wynn family, which is no surprise as they were historically one of the most powerful families, not only in the Conwy valley, but in north Wales. One of the most intriguing memorials in the chapel is the ornate stone coffin of Prince Llywelyn Fawr who died in 1240. His body was initially buried in his abbey at Conwy but was moved up river to Maenan Abbey in 1284 until finally moved to Llanrwst by the Wynn's after the Dissolution. It is perhaps fitting that this empty coffin now rests in the heart of what was Llywelyn's favourite territory. In close proximity to the church are the old almshouses founded by Sir John Wynn of Gwydir in 1610–12. The town's square once boasted a market hall, built in 1661 and rebuilt in the eighteenth century. It was an impressive two-storey stone structure. In spite of it being the town's focal point for over three hundred years, it was deemed necessary to demolish this historic building in order to ensure that traffic flowed smoothly through the town. Fortunately other old buildings have not suffered the same fate. As one leaves the square the old stone bridge with its three graceful arches sits comfortably over the river Conwy. Dated 1636, tradition claims it to be the work of Inigo Jones. Although there is no known record of his having any association with the town, he could have been linked to some work completed for Sir Richard

A Watkin Owen long-case clock. [WAW]

The mansion, Gwydir Castle, photographed before the Great War. [WAW]

Wynn of Gwydir Castle, which is a short distance from the bridge on the other side of the river. This Tudor mansion, built in 1559, was practically razed to the ground by a fire in the 1920s and has been in private ownership over many years. The present owners, however, have sought to restore it to its former glory and it is well worth a visit.

Before crossing the old bridge and taking the A470 to Betws-y-Coed, it is worth making the short journey from Gwydir Castle along the B5106 to Trefriw which boasts a 150-year-old working woollen mill and the Trefriw Wells Spa which dates back to Roman times. It was the soldiers of the XX Roman legion garrisoned at *Canovium* (Caerhun), three miles north of Trefriw who discovered the spa water whilst prospecting for minerals in the mountains above the Conwy Valley. They were so impressed with the special properties of the water that they excavated three short tunnels, converting the spring water into shallow wells in which they could bathe and feel the benefit of the waters' medicinal and healing properties. The wells continued to be used by local inhabitants until a landslip blocked the entrance to the wells. In 1733, the cave was re-excavated and people began to bathe in the waters once again. As people from further afield than the Conwy Valley heard of the medicinal qualities of the Trefriw waters, a local landowner, seeing its commercial possibilities, built a Bath House in 1743 which was better able to cater for the ever-growing number of people visiting the spa.

In Victorian times, visiting a spa was a popular pastime for the landed gentry and wealthy entrepreneurs. Trefriw Wells and Spa became the place to visit especially around 1874 when the Victorian pump room and bathhouse were built. Small ships brought people up river from Conwy to the quay in Trefriw whilst others travelled by rail to Llanrwst and then by horse-drawn carriages, crossing a purpose-built bridge over the river to Trefriw. It was during this time that the spa water was sold commercially. The spa's popularity continued throughout the Edwardian era, and by 1910, it was one of the leading social centres during the summer months. As a result, Trefriw prospered and hotels and houses were built. There were a number of shops and many other facilities for the growing number of visitors. During the First World War, however, the spa's popularity declined and although the water was still bottled and sold all over the world by mail order, the Wells complex fell into disrepair between 1959 and 1971, and lost its popularity as a tourist attraction. In the late 1970s, people became interested once again in natural health remedies and the spa was restored and opened to the public once again.

In spite of the spa's demise and recovery, one industry has survived for over 150 years. The Trefriw Woollen Mill is still weaving its traditional Welsh bedspreads, tweeds, travelling rugs and tapestry quilts on machines which are forty to fifty years old and now generated by the mill's own electricity. Visitors can see the cloth being woven and view the hydro-electric turbines which power the looms. The mill has a shop selling its own products and others sourced from around Britain and further afield, as well as a tearoom where very tasty homemade cakes and light meals can be enjoyed. Trefriw mill is the last remaining working woollen mill in the Conwy Valley. Bought in 1859 by Thomas Williams, it had been operating as a *pandy* (fulling mill) for over thirty years where the fast running water of the river Crafnant drove the water wheels and was also used to wash the wool. Together with the Wells Spa and its woollen mill, Trefriw has once again become a popular tourist attraction giving visitors an insight into the history of the lovely Conwy Valley.

Leaving Trefriw and returning to Llanrwst to cross the river via the town's old bridge, a small stone cottage, Tu Hwnt i'r Bont (meaning beyond the river), sits on the river bank. Once used as a courthouse, it still retains many of its early seventeenth century features and is now in the care of the National Trust. Its popular tearooms are very busy during the summer.

The main route, the A470, from Llanrwst to Betws-y-Coed provides a good view of the forest-clad valley slopes with several old farms on either side of the road, many of them dating from the seventeenth century and retaining features from that time. Soon the road joins the A5, and the forest and mountains seem ever closer. Another bridge, the Waterloo Bridge, takes the road over the river Conwy and into Betws-y-Coed. This graceful iron bridge, built in 1815, the year of the battle of Waterloo, is a fine example of Thomas Telford's work.

To many visitors, Betws-y-Coed is the gateway to Snowdonia. From here, it is convenient to walk the hills and climb the mountains. Fishing and other water sports are also popular as the village is close to the point where three rivers meet – the Conwy, the Lledr and the Llugwy. Having crossed the Waterloo Bridge, the village of grey-stone houses, hotels and shops, with their blue-slate roofs, borders the busy A5 with a backcloth of forest greenery. The river Llugwy rushes through the village on its way to join the Conwy. Near the railway station is the ancient church of St Michael, dating from the fourteenth century although probably an earlier church stood on the same site. Evidence of this is the presence of the font inside the church which dates from the thirteenth century. Also inside the church is an interesting seventeenth-century wooden altar and pulpit with fragments of stained glass dating from the late fifteenth and early sixteenth century in the east and west windows. In the chancel is a recumbent effigy of an armoured knight, believed to be that of Gruffydd ap Dafydd Goch whose lineage goes back to Llywelyn ap Gruffydd, the last of the native Welsh princes. Near the church is a handsome suspension foot-bridge which crosses the river Conwy, leading to a scenic walk along the river bank. Beside the bridge, the still deep waters of the river are known as Church Pool.

Betws-y-Coed has been a focal point for travellers since early times with ancient trackways, Roman roads and packhorse trails criss-crossing the moorland and mountain passes around the village. For the enthusiastic hill-walker, it is still possible to follow many of these routes today. In 1844, an artist colony was established here by David Cox and other well known Victorian landscape painters such as J. M .W. Turner. David Cox first came to the area in 1804–06 and was so inspired by its beauty that he returned on a regular basis and encouraged other artists to share and enjoy the great diversity of landscape which can be found within a radius of a few miles. Over time, a number of artists set up their studios here and the colony was born. The Royal Oak Hotel has in its possession a painting by David Cox of an oak tree that was in the hotel grounds at the time. It was originally placed outside the hotel, but as its value increased it was placed in the reception area, where it still hangs. There is no doubt that this influx of artists brought prominence to the village and there is still a woodland on the outskirts of the village called Artists' Wood.

It was the coming of the railway which resulted in Betws-y-Coed becoming a major centre for tourists. It was at this time when all the hotels, boarding houses and all the other buildings relating to tourism, were erected. Today, they continue to meet the needs of visitors from the four corners of the world. As Betws-y-Coed is a village set up along river banks, it naturally has a number of bridges. In the centre of the village is Pont-y-Pair bridge (the bridge of the cauldron) crossing the river Llugwy, so named because of the deep pool of foaming water which can be seen below the bridge, especially after a heavy rainfall. The first bridge was built here in 1468 by a stone mason from Bala, with a second bridge being added alongside the original in order to provide more width. As in the case of Llanrwst bridge, it is thought that Inigo Jones was involved in the design of the second bridge, but again there is no evidence to support this. But no matter who was responsible there is no doubt that Pont-y-Pair is a fine example of fifteenth-century stone bridge building.

From this old bridge it is possible to enjoy several riverside walks. One such walk begins in the car park on the far side of the bridge from where the path meanders through the trees, alongside the river bank, as the river rushes over the glistening rocks. Here and there still, deep pools interrupt the flow, allowing occasional fish to leap out of the water and create its own ripples on the water. For the energetic walker, this path continues on towards the most popular feature of Betws-y-Coed – the Swallow Falls – which attracts visitors all the year round. Before reaching the falls, however, another interesting bridge crosses the river. Known as the Miner's Bridge, it is a solid wooden structure, rather like a ship's gangplank, securely anchored to the steep cliff face on either side of the river. The original bridge was constructed by miners who lived in the now deserted villages of Rhiwddolian and Pentre Du, high up on the moorland to the south of the river. These bleak moorlands, with their sparse vegetation, did not encourage full-time farming so the men sought employment elsewhere to supplement the family income and many made their way to the slate quarries in Blaenau Ffestiniog. They would walk over the mountain to Pont-y-Pant in the Lledr valley and get the train to Ffestiniog, making the return journey at the end of their shift. Others

Pont-y-Pair, Betws-y-Coed. [WAW]

would walk down into the Llugwy valley and cross over the river to walk up the steep, wooded slopes to work the lead mines which were scattered around these uplands. The Miner's Bridge made their river crossing easier, as the waters of the river can be particularly deep and turbulent at this point, increased at times by heavy rainfall and melting snow from the surrounding mountains. This river crossing, long before the bridge was built, was on the old Roman route – Sarn Helen – which crossed the mountain from Dolwyddelen in the Lledr valley to Caerhun in the Conwy valley.

The Swallow Falls, were originally known by their Welsh name – Rhaeadr Ewynnol – which translated means the foaming water. The Welsh word *ewynnol* is, however, very similar to the Welsh word *wennol* meaning swallow (bird) and at some point someone misheard or mispronounced the word *ewynnol*, referring to the falls as *Rhaeadr y Wennol* which was duly translated to Swallow Falls, a name which is now used by both locals and visitors alike. As the waterfall is situated just below the A5, most visitors arrive here by car and are able to park in the ample car park of the Swallow Falls Hotel, which is opposite the entrance to the waterfall. A steep path and steps lead down to a platform which provides a fine view of the falls where the river Llugwy surges and foams over rocks eventually dropping down in a series of cascades of foaming water. When in full spate, the rush and roar of the water can be exhilarating, if somewhat overwhelming. But in the summer months, if the volume of the cascading water is not as great, the falls appear as a glistening skein of silver sparkling in the sunlight. It is no wonder that this beautiful setting has drawn artists, writers and poets over the years and provided an opportunity for so many others, seeking to escape their hectic lives, to observe nature in all its glory, described so vividly by the traveller George Borrow:

The Fall of the Swallow is not a majestic single fall, but a succession of small ones. First there is a number of little foaming torrents, bursting through the rocks about twenty yards above the promontory on which I stood. Then came two beautiful rolls of white water, dashing into a pool a little way above the promontory; then there is a swirl of water round its

Swallow Falls, c.1910. [WAW]

corner into a pool below on its right, black as death and seemingly of great depth; then a rush through a very narrow outlet into another pool, from which the water clamours away down the glen. Such is the Rhaeadr y Wennol or Swallow Fall; called so from the rapidity with which the waters rush and skip along.

Leaving Betws-y-Coed, its waterfall and other varied attractions, the A5 route continues on its way through the Llugwy valley, its scenery continuing to surprise and amaze as the presence of the majestic mountains come into view, confirming the closeness of the Snowdonia heartland. In spite of the road twisting its way through wooded slopes, now and again a break in the trees gives a glimpse of the spectacular peak of Moel Siabod rising up into the clouds, giving a taste of what is to come. A few miles out of Betws, squatting low beneath a canopy of trees is Y Tŷ Hyll (The Ugly House). Despite its name it draws many visitors to take a closer look. Dating from the fifteenth century, it is known in Welsh as a *tŷ nos* (house of the night), its outer walls constructed of huge boulders placed, it seems, on top of each other with no regular pattern, an accepted method in many areas of Wales. It was a custom that, if someone was able to build a house in one night – between dusk and dawn – and ensure that smoke was rising from the chimney before sunrise, then the builder gained possession of the house and the land it stood on. This particular house was often used by Irish drovers taking their cattle to the English markets.

From 'Tŷ Hyll' the road continues on towards Capel Curig with the river Llugwy alongside and the impressive bulk of Moel Siabod ahead. Before long, a cluster of wooden buildings, the Welsh Brigade Training School appears, situated between the road and the river. Behind the school, on the other side of the river is the site of Caer Llugwy, a Roman camp which was a strategic military camp from 100 A.D. to 140 A.D. and an important link in the chain of similar camps in north Wales. Caer Llugwy was well situated, defended by the river on three sides, and had a direct link with the Roman fort of Segontium (Caernarfon) in the west. It also provided a link between the Roman camp at Tomen-y-Mur (near Trawsfynydd) and Caerhun (in the Conwy valley). The approach to Capel Curig is flanked by two hotels – the Ty'n-y-Coed and Cobden's. Originally coaching inns, they have provided hospitality over many decades. Soon the first glimpses of Yr Wyddfa – Snowdon – appears on the skyline, it is this close proximity that has made the village a centre for mountain climbers and hill walkers alike. The village is situated on an important junction where the A4086 from Llanberis and Beddgelert meets up with the A5 before the latter makes its way through Nant Ffrancon towards the coast and Anglesey, to end its journey in

The Ugly House. [WAW]

Holyhead. But it is the mountains, which suddenly surround the traveller at this point, that stimulate a desire to see more and Snowdonia does not disappoint. The Glyders rise up ahead, the Carneddi to the right and to the left Dyffryn Mymbyr with its twin lakes making a perfect introduction to the Snowdon Horseshoe ahead. Capel Curig is a rather scattered community, its centre being a cluster of houses and shops with the ancient church dedicated to the Celtic saint, Curig, on the bank above the river Llugwy. Considered by many as one of the oldest tourist centres in the land, it provides nearby lakes for fishermen and canoeists, high mountains for walkers and challenging rock faces for climbers.

Leaving the A5, the A4086 heads towards Dyffryn Mymbyr. A short distance from Capel Curig is Plas-y-Brenin, once a hotel, now the National Mountain Centre providing a variety of outdoor activities. Originally built as the Capel Curig Inn in 1801 by Lord Penrhyn who felt it was ideally placed above the twin lakes of Dyffryn Mymbyr below to benefit from the developing tourist trade, it was later re-named the Royal Hotel as it became popular with royalty, Princess Victoria having stayed there as a guest. The view from here down the valley and across the lakes is probably the most photographed scene in all of Snowdonia, taking in the spectacular, panoramic view of the Snowdon Horseshoe. Thomas Pennant wrote: 'Snowdon and all his sons, Crib Coch, Crib-y-Ddysgl, Lliwedd-yr-Aran, and many others, here burst at once full in view, and make this far the finest approach to our boasted Alps.'

Irrespective of the season, the journey down Dyffryn Mymbyr is always memorable. Isolated sheep farms can be seen hugging the hillside, this is truly hill-farming country. Situated about midway along this valley is Dyffryn Mymbyr farm, made famous in Thomas Firbank's best-selling book *I Bought a Mountain* in which he describes Welsh hill-farming in this beautiful but unforgiving landscape. At the head of the valley is Pen-y-Gwryd with its hotel made famous in the early 1950s when the team members of the British Everest Expedition, led by Sir John Hunt, stayed here whilst completing their rigorous training on the

Facing: Looking along Dyffryn Mymbyr towards Snowdon
(the left-hand of the three main peaks in the distance). [WAW]

difficult local mountain routes in preparation for the first successful ascent of Everest. Not only did their success have an impact across the world, but also on this small corner of Snowdonia which saw an increase in climbers wanting to test their skills against the mountains. The hotel, standing 900 feet above sea level, is not very old, having only been built in the nineteenth century when mountaineering was beginning to become a popular sport and past-time. It is interesting to note, however, that Pen-y-Gwryd was considered a strategic site long before the nineteenth century when the Romans established a transit camp here for their legions who marched between Caerhun and Segontium. Situated on a rise, opposite the hotel above the small Pen-y-Gwryd lake, a stony bank covered in thick turf is all that remains of their camp.

Today there are five main recognised routes which lead to the summit of Yr Wyddfa. Whichever route is chosen, it is essential that the right clothing and equipment are used, that one's route is known by someone and that possible weather changes are taken into consideration. It will also require a sustained effort and a respect for the mountain, but when the summit is finally reached it can prove to be an unforgettable experience. The words of an old Welsh rhyme summarises this well:

> Hawdd yw dwedyd, 'Dacw'r Wyddfa',
> Nid eir trosti ond yn ara'.

Which roughly translated means – 'It is easy to say, "There's Snowdon", but you'll only go over her very slowly'.

Two of the most popular routes start at Pen-y-Pass which is situated on the main road from Pen-y-Gwryd to Llanberis – the Pyg Track and the Miner's Track. The Pyg Track (name taken from Pen-y-Gwryd and not from the animal) is very rocky and calls for quite a bit of hard climbing right from the start, the Miner's Track, however, gives a more leisurely start and the broad expanse of scenery which opens up along this ancient trackway is quite majestic. Before long, the small Llyn Teyrn appears and the path begins to rise up gradually towards Llyn Llydaw which is sheltered by the seemingly black rock face of Lliwedd to the left and Crib Coch rising steeply to the right. Here the track crosses a causeway and

The Pen-y-Gwryd Hotel. [WAW]

continues along the banks of Llyn Llydaw, bringing one well and truly
into the mountains. It is surprising to see the remains of old copper-
mining buildings clinging to the steep slopes around and above the lake.
The mines were worked from the middle of the eighteenth century until
1915 and one can only imagine the hardship felt by the miners working
in this challenging environment particularly in the depths of winter. Here
they would live for a week in the primitive stone cabins on the edge of
Llyn Teyrn and return home, over the mountains, to neighbouring
villages at the weekend. Above Llyn Llydaw is Bwlch y Saethau (the Pass
of Arrows), which appears as a dip on the ridge between Lliwedd and Yr
Wyddfa. Legend has it that King Arthur fought his last battle here, dying
from a fatal arrow wound, hence the name of the pass. His knights are
said to be asleep in a cave on the face of Lliwedd waiting for their king to
return.

From Llyn Llydaw the track becomes a steep path rising up to the
shores of Llyn Glaslyn with the mountain's cliff face rising steeply,
practically vertically, to its summit, giving the impression that there is no
way out beyond this lake. The still waters of the lake belie its depth and
are said to be haunted, but it is the colour of the water, a deep blue-green
which gives it an added unreal appearance and also gives the lake its

name. Glaslyn when translated, means Blue Lake, the colour of its water being the result of the copper deposits which have flowed into it from the surrounding streams. The lake is also linked to an old Welsh legend which adds to its rather mysterious appearance; it is allegedly, the home of a water monster in the shape of a huge beaver-like creature. This monster, it is said, lived in a pool in the Conwy valley near Betws-y-Coed known as Beaver's Pool (close to the Waterloo Bridge there is still a house called Beaver's Grove). Possessing supernatural powers this monster would, from time to time, flood the valley, ruining crops and drowning cattle. No matter how the valley dwellers attempted to destroy it, their efforts were unsuccessful and it was decided that the only way to rid the valley of this creature was to remove it and deposit it in a lake high up in the nearby mountains. It was known that the monster was partial to beautiful maidens and volunteers from the valley community were asked to step forward to act as a decoy. One brave young woman agreed to do this and when the monster was enticed out of its pool, overcome by the young woman's beauty, it was surrounded and tied up with the strongest chains available. These were then harnessed to a team of mighty oxen. As the monster came out of its daze, it struggled so much that it fell back into the pool, but the oxen held steadfast and gradually dragged it out again. Their mammoth task now began, and the creature which had caused so much devastation was hauled through the valley, across the hills and eventually up the mountainside being finally deposited in the deep waters of Llyn Glaslyn.

The path from Llyn Glaslyn rises steeply, zig-zagging between the rocks, eventually joining up with the Pyg Track, the crest of Y Grib Goch rising directly above and the rocky face of Crib-y-Ddysgl ahead. As the path ahead becomes very rocky and sometimes slippy, great care and considerable energy is required to progress upwards. The effort to do this is well-rewarded for, when the final precipitous slope reaches the ridge of Crib-y-Ddysgl, the panorama which opens up to both the right and the left is stunning. The lakes of Llydaw and Glaslyn sparkle below with the Miner's Track, ribbon-like, winding its way around their shores and the dark, steep, rocky sides of Lliwedd providing a dramatic backcloth. In

The Mountain Railway track runs close to the edge at Clogwyn. [WAW]

another direction, the eye sweeps down into Cwm Glâs which eventually reaches down to the Llanberis Pass below. At this point the impression is of feeling on top of the world and the final effort required to reach Snowdon's summit does not overwhelm and the path becomes clearer, following the track of the Snowdon Mountain Railway, eventually arriving at Hafod Eryri, situated just below the summit rock, a building which only recently replaced the rather shabby 'hotel' which stood on this extraordinary site. From the summit, at a height of 1085 metres, the views of the landscape are overwhelming. Perhaps surprisingly, therefore, this is a busy place, particularly during the summer when the railway brings up many thousnads of tourists to amaze at the spectacular panorama of mountains and lakes. Built in 1896, the rack and pinion rail system has carried millions to the top of the mountain over the years. To appreciate Yr Wyddfa's true magnificence, however, you need to stand on its summit crag on a quiet, clear day and take in what is regarded as one of the best views in Britain.

The expanse of mountain and landscape is overwhelming and yet the immediate views are also fantastic. Lliwedd with its craggy and precipitous cliffs reaches out from the summit, a narrow path clinging to its ridge, far below the lakes of Glaslyn and Llydaw with Cwm Dyli opening out towards Nant Gwynant. Beyond Dyffryn Mymbyr, Moel Siabod casts its shadow over the twin lakes and on the far horizon Cadair Idris stands out as a lone sentinel. Between Crib Coch and Crib-y-Ddysgl the Glyders rise up, with a glimpse of Carnedd Llywelyn and Pen yr Oleu Wen appearing beyond. To the south-west, Moel Hebog's clear outline rises above Beddgelert, and the compact, neat shape of Mynydd Mawr to the north. If the weather holds out, Llyn Cwellyn with Moel Eilio behind, leads the eye further to Anglesey and the sea. The ultimate reward is to see Ireland, the Isle of Man and the peaks of the Lake District on the far horizon.

Some would argue that Yr Wyddfa – Snowdon – is the most wondrous of the Seven Wonders, it is probably in many ways the most spectacular. The other six 'wonders', however, are each special in their own way and cannot be isolated from the environments that surround them, to visit them all is in fact, a wondrous journey.

Bibliography

Aston, Steve, *Classic Walks in Wales* (Promotional Reprint Company, 1995).

Berry, David, *Llangollen & the Dee Valley – Local Walks* (Kittiwake, 2000).

Bingley, Rev. W., *North Wales* (Denbighshire County Council edition).

Borrow, George, *Wild Wales* (Bridge Books, 2009).

Brown, Colin & Mary, *The Clockmakers of Llanrwst*, (Bridge Books, 1993).

—— *Chirk Castle* (The National Trust).

Emery, Gordon, *Curious Clwyd – Volumes 1 & 2* (Gordon Emery, Vol 2, 1996).

      Guide to the Maelor Way (Gordon Emery, 1991 & 1996).

      & Roberts, John, *Day Walks – Vale of Llangollen* (Walkways, 1991).

—— *Erddig* (National Trust).

Fletcher, H. L. V., *The Queen's Wales – North Wales* (Hodder & Stoughton, 1955).

Gardner, Don, *The Vagabond book of South Snowdonia* (*Cambrian News*).

Griffiths, Eric, *Philip Yorke I (1743–1804) Squire of Erthig* (Bridge Books, 1995).

Gregory, Donald, *Wales before 1536 – A Guide* (Gwasg Carreg Gwalch, 1993).

Grindle, Jim, *Circular Walks in North Eastern Wales* (Gwasg Carreg Gwalch, 1999).

Harrison, Sunter, *Erbistock* (Privately published, 1988).

Hart, E. K. Mortimer, *The Conwy Valley and the lands of History* (2nd ed, Landmark Publishing, 2004).

Hubbard, Edward, *The Buildings of Wales – Clwyd* (Penguin Books/ University of Wales Press, 1986).

Jenner, Lorna, *Walking in the Vale of Clwyd & the Denbigh Moors* (Mara Books, 2000).

Jones, J. Colin, *Gresford Village & Church & Royal Marford* (Privately published, 1995).

Jones, J. Graham, *A History of Wales – A pocket guide* (University of Wales Press, 1990).

Jones, Jane A. Lewis, *The History of Llanarmon Dyffryn Ceiriog & Tregeiriog* (Jane Lewis Jones) n.d.

Jones, Geoffrey A., & Williams, W. Alister, *Images of Wrexham, the County Borough through the camera lens* (Bridge Books, 2007)

Jones, Ivor Wynne, *Wilder Wales – Out and About in North Wales* (Gwasg Carreg Gwalch, 2001).

Lewis [ed.], Jennie, *The Hidden Places of the Welsh Borders* (M&M Publishing, Altrincham).

Lewis, Pete, *Wat's Dyke Way Heritage Trail* (Alyn Books, 2008).

Lomax, Jeff, *Offa's Dyke Path. Volume 1 – Prestatyn to Welshpool* (Mara Publications, 1998).

Lowe, Raymond, *Lost Houses In and Around Wrexham* (Landmark Publishing, 2002).

Maddern, Ralph, *Walk Snowdonia* (Focus Publications, 1981).

Morton, H. V., *In Search of Wales* (Methuen, 1932).

Jones, John Price, *Oswestry Parish Church* (Llanforda Press, 1992).

Pennant, Thomas, *A Tour in Wales* (Bridge Books, 1991 edition).

Powell, John, *Holt & its records through the centuries* (Privately published, 1982).

Rees, Cynthia, *A History of the Parish of Marchwiel* (Bridge Books, 1993).

Roberts, Dewi, *The Land of Old Renown – George Borrow in Wales* (Gwasg Carreg Gwalch, 1997).

Senior, Michael, *Portrait of North Wales* (Gwasg Carreg Gwalch, 2001).

Sherratt, Gordon, *An Illustrated History of Llangollen* (Ceiriog Press, 2000).

Tranter, John, *Walks in and Around the Berwyn Mountains* (Gwasg Carreg Gwalch, 1999).

———— *A Visitors Guide to Llansilin* (Llansilin Local History Society 1989).

Watkin, Isaac, *Oswestry, with an account od its old houses, shops. etc and some of their occupants* (1920, reprinted by Bridge Books, 2006).

Williams, W. Alister, *The Encyclopædia of Wrexham* (Bridge Books, 2001).